You Were Born Rich

BOB PROCTOR

YOU WERE BORN RICH

Now You Can Discover and Develop Those Riches

LifeSuccess Productions
2921 W. Culver Street, #1
Phoenix, AZ 85009
800-871-9715
800-317-9679 fax
www.bobproctor.com

Cover Design: Van Crosby

Printed and bound in the United States of America

ISBN 0-9656264-1-5

10 9 8 7 6 5 4 3 2 1

**DEDICATED TO
LINDA**

who brought the sun from the south
with her and willingly shared it with
Brian, Colleen and Raymond.

One And Only You

Every single blade of grass,
And every flake of snow—
Is just a wee bit different ...
There's no two alike, you know.

From something small, like grains of sand,
To each gigantic star
All were made with THIS in mind:
To be just what they are!

How foolish then, to imitate—
How useless to pretend!
Since each of us comes from a MIND
Whose ideas never end.

There'll only be just ONE of ME
To show what I can do—
And you should likewise feel very proud,
There's only ONE of YOU.

That is where it all starts
With you, a wonderful
unlimited human being.

James T. Moore

Introduction

Every human being has been "**Born Rich**;" it's just that most people are temporarily a little short of money! This book has been written in an attempt to bridge the gap between where you currently are and where you want to be. Step by step, chapter by chapter, it will help you piece together the puzzle we most often refer to as "**life**," so you can build a picture of prosperity in your mind, and then go on to create that prosperity in your life. Indeed, life is very much like the Rubic's Cube because we have all the right pieces, and all the right colors, but it is a frustrating, never-ending process, trying to get them to fit together. Inevitably, it seems, there are always at least one or two pieces we have left out.

As you journey through this book, you will soon become very aware I am not telling you anything you do not already know. I am just expressing the ideas in an organized, coherent manner, which will enable you to achieve the results you have desired since you were first able to think. Every day, all over the world, millions of "dreamers" purchase lottery tickets, wishing for someone to fortuitously pick their names, and drop a fortune into their laps. These people never seem to understand that the real joy in life comes not from having money handed to them on a "silver platter," but from going out and actually earning it themselves. Moreover, if the truth were known to you, you would realize that you already have the ability to achieve those things which you presently only dream about.

Let this book prove to be your Alladin's Lamp.

You have, in your hands, something which you have been searching for. **This is a plan—a very simple plan—that will take you from where you are, to where you want to be.** It is actually a deceptively simple plan. But do not let its apparent simplicity deceive you, because each chapter contains an idea which will prove to be of enormous value. These ideas are extremely effective. I have personally put each and every one of them to a test over the past quarter of a century. I have watched thousands of people, who have attended my seminars, put these ideas to a test as well. I can tell you, therefore, from both my first and secondhand experiences, the results in many cases have been extraordinary.

For example, individuals with barely enough resources to meet their basic needs have become very wealthy. Others, who had pressing problems which caused them to be unhappy and depressed, have literally transformed themselves into happy, well-balanced individuals.

Now **you** have the opportunity to put these ideas to the supreme test, in your own life. What is it that you want? **Know you can have it—you can have all of the things you want—**but you must clearly understand and apply all of the ideas I am about to present to you. No amount of reading or memorizing will give you the success you desire. **It is only the understanding and application of right-thinking that counts.** So, regardless of what I, or anyone else, might say, you are going to have to prove these ideas for yourself.

I could have filled this book with scientific data,

showing you—in black and white—exhaustive studies documenting the fact that these ideas actually do work. However, other than possibly satisfying the analytical side of your mind, that sort of information would be of little practical use to you. Although I do use many examples in the following pages which describe how individuals, or possibly families, have put these ideas to work and have explained the benefits which they have derived, I have deliberately omitted any scientific research, as I have found that it serves little purpose, from a practical, or result-oriented, point of view. It will only slow you down and possibly cloud your thinking.

This book has been written in such a way that it actually maps out a mental course for you to take to reach any objective that you would like to reach. You can journey from one chapter to the next, each successive chapter lifting you to a greater awareness of yourself—your true self—and of your true abilities. You must, however, keep in the forefront of your mind one important fact: the rewards which you will receive in this life, material or psychic, will not come to you because of your potential but, rather, because of your performance.

Come with me and enjoy a sneak preview of the journey which you are about to take. In the first chapter, "Me And Money," we start to see what this elusive stuff called "money" actually is. We begin to relate to money as we should, and we develop an understanding of why all great thinking people burn a basic principle deep into the recesses of their mind: that is, "we should love people, and use money."

We also find out what happens to anyone who is careless enough to get that equation reversed. This chapter will help you realize there is, in point of fact, no sin in great wealth. On the contrary, it is your duty to become wealthy.

The second chapter, "How Much Is Enough," will help you take a careful inventory of your thoughts and your true financial situation. You will learn how to decide how much is enough for you. You will discover that you should have the amount of money you need, to provide you with the things you want, and to live in the style you choose.

When this decision has been made, you will be prepared to march into chapter three, "The Image-Maker." You will gain the awareness that your entire life is governed by images. It necessarily follows, then, that you should be acutely aware of the images you are building in your mind and you should also be aware of the necessity of building these images which will produce the results that will move you onward and upward, toward your desired destination. You will begin to understand that you are, in truth, a co-creator. Make certain that you often review what your responsibility is, in your co-creative partnership.

Chapter four, "Let Go And Let God," helps you develop a strong faith based on a deep understanding. It will assist you in freely letting go of your image, turning it over to the power within you, so that the power itself can go to work and begin to materialize in physical results, as an exact replica of your mental image.

The next chapter, "Expect An Abundance," will prove to be a mind-expanding experience. The word "expectation" will take on a brand new meaning for you and you will witness the awesome power invoked by this mind-set.

"The Law Of Vibration And Attraction," clears up many question marks that have been in our minds for years. It becomes evident why some people keep attracting what they do not want, while others attract exactly what they do want. You will learn how to magnetize yourself to the good that you desire.

"The Risk-Takers" chapter clearly explains that there is absolutely no compensation for playing it safe. It is essential that you first step out, before you can begin to move toward the destination you have chosen for yourself.

The real winners in life are, more often than not, only two or three percent more effective than those who lose. "The Razor's Edge" chapter clearly illustrates this point. You will quickly understand that you can be every bit as effective as anyone you read about or even hear about. Feelings of inferiority, as well as any doubts you may be entertaining relative to your capability, will quickly fall by the wayside and be left far behind, as you near your destination.

As you come around the final turn on your road to achievement, you will be cautioned not to look back. The "Don't Think In Reverse" chapter will quickly clear up the question of why some people keep getting the same results, year after year. This illustrates one of the most basic, and yet one of the most important, rules governing success in life.

As we go racing down the home stretch, "The Vacuum Law Of Prosperity" shows us how to open all of the doors, that will enable the good that we seek to come to us from all sides. This is not only a rewarding law, but a truly enjoyable one for you to learn. It will help pull all of the other ideas together, to complete your picture and get you to your desired destination safely and on schedule.

Before you begin, let me caution you once again, that reading and memorizing will never "make it happen" for you. It is only understanding and application of the right ideas that will produce the results you desire. Think about each idea very closely. They are all simple and easy to understand, but you must act on them. Keep this book with you. Continually review it, and you will begin to see evidence of everything that is explained in it in your material world. This entire book has been prepared with the sincere hope that you will enjoy every step of your journey into a truly new way of living.

Bob Proctor

TABLE OF CONTENTS

*Those who know the truth
learn to love it.
Those who love the truth
learn to live it.*

Chapter 1

ME
AND
MONEY

ME AND MONEY

The Edgewater Beach Hotel

In 1923, at the Edgewater Beach Hotel in Chicago, eight of the world's wealthiest financiers met. These eight men controlled more money than the United States' government at that time. They included:

The president of the largest independent steel company;
The president of the largest gas company;
The greatest wheat speculator;
The president of the New York Stock Exchange;
A member of the President's cabinet;
The greatest "bear" on Wall Street;
The head of the world's greatest monopoly;
The president of the Bank of International Settlement.

Certainly, one would have to admit, that a group of the world's most successful men was gathered in that place; at least, men who had found the secret of "earning money."

Now let's see where these men were twenty-five years later:

The president of the largest independent steel company, Charles Schwab, lived on borrowed money for five years before he died bankrupt.

The president of North America's largest gas

company, Howard Hopson, went insane.

The greatest wheat speculator, Arthur Cutton, died abroad, insolvent.

The president of the New York Stock Exchange, Richard Whitny, was sent to Sing Sing Penitentiary.

A member of the President's cabinet, Albert Fall, was pardoned from prison so he could die at home.

The greatest "bear" on Wall Street, Jesse Livermore, died a suicide.

The head of the greatest monopoly, Ivar Krueger, killed himself.

The president of the Bank of International Settlement, Leon Fraser, also died a suicide.

Each of these men learned well the art of earning money, but it would seem that not one of them had ever learned how to live the "rich life", which was their birthright.

It is stories like this one that have caused many well meaning, but ignorant people to say, "See, I told you it is not good to have a lot of money, it's bad," or, "It just goes to show you that rich people really aren't happy;" but of course, that is just not true. For although these eight men would appear to have "slid off the track," there are many wealthy people who are very happy, and who do a tremendous amount of good with their money; they live healthy, well-balanced lives.

Consider this—money will have a greater influence on your life than almost any other commodity you can think of. Indeed, the sudden loss or acquisition of money will affect your attitude to a tremendous extent. Therefore, you must agree that everyone should have a deep understanding of exactly what money is, and of the laws governing its attraction. Yet, the sad fact is that not one person in ten does. Ninety-five people out of a hundred settle for whatever they get, wishing they had more all the way from the cradle to the casket, never understanding that they could actually have had all they wanted.

Let me digress for a moment—as you journey through this book, you might have a tendency to let your mind wander off, either thinking about someone you know who has earned a great deal of money or possibly about someone who has gone into bankruptcy. But I want to suggest that you attempt to keep focusing only on yourself, because what someone else has or does not have, is not going to affect you and it is your financial situation that you want to improve.

Money Is Important

One of the most prevalent misconceptions concerning money, relates to its importance. For example, how many times have you heard people say in conversation, "Money isn't everything." or "Money isn't important." or "I don't care about money." Well, the people who say these things might not care about money, but I'll bet their car dealer cares about it; their grocer does; and so does the person who holds their mortgage. In truth, there can be no denial of the fact that money is important to any person living in a civilized society. Therefore, to argue that it is not as important as this or that, is absurd. For nothing can take the place of money in the arena in which it is used!

Money Is A Servant

Now that I have affirmed the importance of money, let me backtrack to add this one word of caution— always remember, money is a servant; you are the master. Be very careful not to reverse that equation, because many people of high intelligence have already done so, to their great detriment. Unfortunately, many of these poor souls loved money and used people, which violated one of the most basic laws governing true financial success. You should always love people and use money, rather than the reverse!

Another myth many people like to accept about money is that it only comes as a result of "luck" or "good fortune." For instance, whenever people gather to talk about someone they know who has been financially successful, there is always someone among them who will say, "Harry was just lucky," or "Harry was just in the right place at the right time." But I want to assure you in no uncertain terms, that although "luck" obviously plays some part in financial success, it is never sufficient in and of itself. Money is an effect and it must always be earned. Believe me, there are no free rides in this life and the only people who are making money the easy way either work in the mint or are on their way to jail, if they have not already arrived there. Therefore, always bear in mind that while "good fortune" is a factor in financial success, it must always be coupled with effort and hard work!

Money Must Circulate

A third thing you should know about money is that it is valuable only as long as it is being used. Once it has been taken out of circulation, it becomes as worthless as the "old newspapers" or "empty beer cans" that have been stashed away in the attic. To understand the truth of this principle, consider the following story. On a bookshelf, in my home, I have a silver beer stein that was given to me as a gift for a speech I made. Now, whenever I go into my house, I take all the change from my pockets and put it into the cup. Then, when the cup is almost filled, I give it to one of my children, or one of two young cousins. Each of them takes turns receiving the cup and of course they eagerly anticipate their turn. The point I want you to notice, however, is that while the cup is being filled, the money in it has absolutely no value whatsoever; it just sits there, serving no useful function and not even drawing any interest.

However, as soon as the cup is filled and the money is turned over to one of the kids, it literally "flies into action." For instance, just last week, T. Jay, one of my young cousins, received the money. He immediately took it from my hand, rushed off to a golf school and purchased several golf lessons with his inheritance. Now, I can't honestly say what the golf pro did with the money once he got it, but I do feel fairly safe in saying that he didn't just return it to a cup on his book shelf! No, there really isn't any dispute about it; money is not meant to be taken out of circulation—rather, it is meant to be used, enjoyed and circulated!

This brings me to an even more dramatic illustration of the same principle: namely, the story of "old Mr. Chapman." Mr. Chapman was an elderly gentleman who lived a few doors down the street from our family when I was just a boy. Although there was a tremendous age difference between us, Mr. Chapman and I became fast friends and I often used to watch him pushing his small junk cart up and down the block. You see, Mr. Chapman worked as a junk dealer and he made his living by picking up the things other people had thrown away. As the years went by, however, Mr. Chapman became more and more stooped from his arduous labors and one day, shortly after World War II, he passed away. Since he lived alone and apparently had no close relatives living nearby, the police entered his house to take stock of his possessions. Not surprisingly, they found the house littered with many old furnishings and assorted memorabilia from Mr. Chapman's past. However, much to their amazement, the police also discovered over one hundred thousand dollars ($100,000) in old bills packed in boxes throughout the house!

Quick to pick up on so unusual an occurrence, the *Toronto Daily Star* carried a front-page story the next day about Mr. Chapman, in which it asked the obvious question: why would an individual worth well over $100,000, choose to keep his money stashed away in old boxes strewn haphazardly throughout his house?

Although I was still quite young at the time, I asked myself a similar question: namely, why would a person like Mr. Chapman choose to live like a veritable pauper, when he had so much money at his disposal? He could have used his money for his own enjoyment. He could have invested it to earn a return for himself and to help create jobs for other people; or he could have just deposited it in the bank and earned interest on his money. But instead, he chose to put it in a "jar on the shelf," and he thereby rendered it absolutely useless. No, my friends, there isn't any doubt about it —money is not meant to be hoarded. Rather, it is meant to be used, enjoyed and circulated. So please, whatever you choose to do with your money, don't make the same mistake that poor old Mr. Chapman did!

Please note that when I suggest that money should be kept in circulation, I do not mean it should be squandered. There is a world of difference between those two concepts and if you haven't found out what the difference is yet, I would suggest you find out as soon as possible.

Prosperity Consciousness Exercise

Now that we have touched upon some of the characteristics of money, let us turn briefly to a simple "technique" which you can begin using immediately to start attracting the amount of money you desire. The first thing that I want you to do is to picture yourself, in your mind's eye, sitting in a room with several of your friends. Then, I want you to visualize yourself announcing to them your intention of becoming wealthy; at least, wealthy enough to live the way you choose to live. Now, imagine how that would make you feel. If you are like most people, you would probably feel very uncomfortable. Perhaps you would feel so uncomfortable, that you might even retract what you had said by informing your friends you were only joking. You should understand, however, that people who are wealthy never feel uncomfortable when the subject of money is brought up. "Why don't they," you ask? The most obvious answer would be, because they already have "lots" of it. But that is not the correct answer. You should realize that people don't feel comfortable about money because they have it; they have it because they feel comfortable about it. In other words, one of the reasons that wealthy people have money is that they have developed that state of consciousness we will hereinafter refer to as, a "prosperity consciousness." Therefore, it follows, if we wish to attract money to ourselves, we must begin to foster a prosperity consciousness as well.

The question you should now be asking yourself is this: "How do I go about developing this prosperity consciousness for myself?" Let me explain. The best way to develop a prosperity consciousness is to start seeing yourself, in your mind's eye, already in possession of the amount of money that you desire. The reason this is so is that since the subconscious mind cannot distinguish between the actual possession of money and mere visualization, you will soon become very comfortable with the "idea" of money. As a result, you will start attracting it to yourself.

This may sound like a game you are playing, but let me assure you, it is one of the wisest things you can possibly do. For when you succeed in convincing your subconscious mind that you are wealthy and that it feels good to be wealthy, your subconscious mind will automatically seek ways of making your "imaginary" feelings of wealth manifest themselves in material form.

If these last few lines seem like sheer fantasy to you, just ignore them for the time being and continue reading. We will be dealing with prosperity consciousness at different points in the book and I guarantee you that before you finish this book, those lines will start to make a lot more sense to you.

Fear Not

Now that I have touched upon a "technique" which will help you acquire greater wealth, let me offer this further word of warning. If you want to have money, one thing you should never, never do, is worry about whether or not you will get the money you desire, or whether you will keep it. Let me elaborate.

In the Bible, Job, the great sufferer of biblical times, makes the following remark: "Behold, the thing I fear has come to visit upon me." Now, stop and ask yourself —if you will—what those biblical words mean to those of us concerned about money today. Well, one thing they certainly mean is that if we insist upon constantly worrying about not having enough money, or if we habitually worry about losing the money we do have, then we are absolutely guaranteed not to worry in vain. For just as surely as Job was afflicted by his many maladies, so too shall we be afflicted by the lack or the loss of money.

To take a more contemporary example, let us again consider the tragic case of "poor old Mr. Chapman." As you will recall, he was the elderly gentleman who never spent any of his hard-earned savings. But the question is, "Why didn't he?" Most likely it was because he was afraid that if he spent his money, he would become poor and hence would be forced to live like a pauper. The irony was, however, that because of his fear, he lived like a pauper anyway! Or, to be more biblical about it, "The thing that he feared most came to visit upon him."

In a later chapter you will be given a fuller explanation of the paradox of why we attract into our lives the very things we least desire. But for now, suffice it to say, worrying about money is always extremely counterproductive. This principle holds true, even if you rationalize your worry with the old platitude that you are "just saving a little for a rainy day."

I must put forward one other caveat at this time: if you really want to significantly increase the amount of money you are presently earning, the first thing you must do is learn to pay substantially less attention to what others around you are saying and substantially more attention to what that "quiet voice" that speaks within you, is saying. Put more prosaically: you must strive to become much less susceptible to influences outside of yourself and much more inclined to trust the instincts and feelings that lie within you. Let me elaborate.

Most people who fail to accumulate enough money to live in the style they choose are the same people who are most easily influenced by other people's opinions. For instance, they are often the people who let the writers of economic doom and gloom—whether in the newspapers or on news broadcasts —do their thinking for them. But, as Napoleon Hill pointed out in his great book, *Think and Grow Rich*, opinions are the cheapest commodities on earth. In fact, almost everyone has a flock of them ready to be foisted upon anyone who is willing to accept them. Therefore, if you know you have been unduly influenced in the past by other people's opinions, make up your mind right now— before you read any further—that from here on in, you are going to heed your own counsel, while keeping an attentive ear open for God's counsel. Remember, if you do, there is absolutely no reason why you cannot become financially successful within a very reasonable period of time.

Understanding vs. Memorization

As you read on through the pages in this book, you will develop an ever-increasing awareness of the talents and abilities that lie deep within you. You should realize, that with the proper instruction, you can begin using these undeveloped talents to attract the good that you desire. But let me caution you once again—no amount of reading or memorizing will bring you the success you seek. It is only the understanding and application of the ideas in this book that will make the difference for you. Therefore, don't be in any hurry to finish the book, because a complete reading should not be your objective. As stated previously, understanding and applying what you read is the objective. So if you are able to properly digest only one page a day, that might be all that is necessary for you to arrive at your goal. If you are wondering why this book is meant to be "sipped and tasted," rather than "devoured" at one reading, bear in mind it is based upon over twenty years of careful analysis of the methods of both the very successful and the very unsuccessful.

Strength Through Sharing

One more word of advice. Since very few—if any—people become great at anything by themselves, I would suggest you attempt to find at least one other person with whom you can share and discuss the ideas presented in this book.

Prosperity Consciousness

I believe you will agree it is an observable truth that human beings will never enjoy anything they are not yet consciously aware of. For example, we did not enjoy the luxury of travelling in airplanes at tremendous rates of speed, until the Wright Brothers became consciously aware of "how to fly." Thomas Edison developed the conscious awareness of the moving pictures and introduced us to a brand new form of entertainment. Dr. Jonas Salk became consciously aware of how to develop a serum that would combat the dreadful disease of infantile-paralysis—more commonly referred to as polio—and as a result of Salk's new awareness, you very rarely hear of anyone contracting that disease today. Alexander Graham Bell became consciously aware of how to transmit the human voice over metallic wires and, as a result, we all now enjoy the use of the telephone.

Needless to say, I could go on and on citing example after example. However, the point I want to bring to the forefront of your mind is that these inventions—or the knowledge bringing about these inventions—have always been here. In fact, all the knowledge there ever was or ever will be, is evenly present in all places at all times. But it took an individual to bring those thought-patterns together and form ideas which developed into what we call consciousness, before we could begin to benefit from them.

We are floating in an "ocean" of thought-energy, where all the knowledge there ever was or ever will be, is present. We are also surrounded by abundance. Indeed, everywhere we look in nature, our eyes come in contact with abundance; for nature knows no such thing as "failure." Therefore, there never has been, and there never will be, a lack of anything, except conscious-awareness. But if you are going to begin to penetrate this world of wealth, it is absolutely essential that you begin to think. In other words, you must open your mind to the stream of thought-energy which will create an image, or a consciousness of prosperity, in your mind.

You are well aware there are literally thousands upon thousands of honest, good, hard-working people who labor diligently for their entire stay on this planet, yet never become wealthy. For those individuals, life is a constant grind from sun up until sun down. But the ideas presented on these pages have been put here in the hope they will jar your mind and inspire you to open it up to this new type of thinking.

Consciousness is, and always has been, developed through thinking, and regardless of what your present situation in life may be, if you ever hope to improve it and truly become wealthy—as this book suggests you can—you must begin thinking of prosperity in your mind, now. Not when you finish the book. Not when you finish the chapter. Not tomorrow, next week, next month or next year. It must be done now. Thinking is the highest function of which a human being is capable. Yet, unfortunately, very few people "think." They merely trick themselves into believing that because there is some mental activity taking place in their mind, they are "thinking." But the truth is, most people are simply exercising the mental faculty called "memory." They are playing old movies, so old pictures just keep flashing back on the screen of their mind.

It is imperative that you begin this new way of thinking at this moment, because as you do, every fibre of your being will become filled with this new thought-energy. Your body is comprised of millions upon millions of cells and each one of them is influenced in its movement by thought impulses. So the second you begin entertaining relaxing thoughts, your body becomes relaxed. The instant you begin entertaining worrisome, fearful thoughts, your body becomes rigid and tense. As you begin to hold thoughts of prosperity and begin thinking of yourself as a very wealthy, prosperous individual who is surrounded by an ocean of thought energy, swimming in a sea of plenty, your body and mind will instantly move into a prosperous vibration and you will begin to attract—just like a magnet—everything necessary for you to become wealthy.

I know to the uninitiated, these ideas are just about as bizarre as anything a person could think of. Nevertheless, they are true. For mental awareness of prosperity always precedes wealth in your material world. It is not difficult, therefore, for children today, born into families of great wealth—like the Kennedy's or the Bronfman's—to think these prosperous thoughts and to have this prosperity consciousness, since that is the only type of thinking they were subjected to, right from birth. We say they have been conditioned in, or to, prosperity.

However, the majority of people have not been born into that kind of an environment and so they were not surrounded by that type of thinking. We must, therefore, develop an understanding of:

1)   how we have been conditioned,
2)   why we are getting the results we are getting, and
3)   how we can change our way of thinking or our conditioning.

That is not an easy thing to do. It takes much discipline. It takes a tremendous desire. It takes a lot of diligent effort, which is the probable reason so few people ever actually change. Yet I want you to know that regardless of how difficult it may be, it can be done and it can be done in a relatively short period of time. The compensation you will receive for your effort will delight you. I know because I have done it and I know many, many other people who have done the same thing. Now it is necessary for you to do it.

The very fact that you have picked up and started reading this book is all the proof you will ever need, that you truly do have a desire to change. Moreover, there is a way—a sure way—for you to receive your desired good, and this book will outline the way for you.

There Is Real Power Within You

Below the level of your consciousness is the great treasury of your subconscious mind and that is the part of your personality we want to begin to influence through our new thought-patterns. In order to make the issue definite and concrete, consider the following statement: any idea, plan or purpose may be planted in the subconscious mind by repetition of thought empowered by faith and expectancy. You might be asking: "Can this statement be demonstrated to be true through experimentation and observation or, is there any known method or technique by which the proof may be secured, and if there is such a method or technique, is it available to everyone?" These questions can all be answered with an emphatic yes. As you read, test, and experiment with the ideas that will come to you in the following pages, you will answer all of these questions for yourself. And, it is necessary that you answer them for yourself, because as human beings, we will not truly believe something until we actually discover it for ourselves.

This book was written in the sincere hope that it would lead you to the many discoveries that lie within you by the repetition of these prosperity ideas. You must begin to see money as an obedient, diligent servant, that you can employ to earn more money, and that you can use to provide services far beyond the service that you could ever physically provide. It is necessary that you feel comfortable when you talk about money, because you have truly been "Born Rich." You have all the mental tools necessary to attract the thoughts you are surrounded by, to create the consciousness that you must create in order for you to have the wealth you choose to have. Lack and limitation can only exist when we make room for them in our minds. But prosperity consciousness knows no lack and no limitation. Resolve to completely remove the lid from your marvelous mind, with respect to your own earning-ability, and understand that the wealth you are seeking is—and always has been—seeking you in return. So open wide the doors of your conscious mind now, and begin to receive it.

Mental Money

Begin immediately to play a mental game with yourself—get into the habit of visualizing yourself in the possession of great wealth. Think of some of the things you would do with that money and then mentally start doing them. Since your subconscious mind cannot tell the difference between actually doing something and visualizing yourself doing it, this exercise will very quickly help you to develop a prosperity consciousness. Remember, it is an absolute law of your being, that you must have something mentally before you will ever have it physically!

Also understand that everyone talks to themselves mentally—in fact, some people even do it out loud. Therefore, whenever you are carrying on your private conversation with yourself, always talk about how good it feels to be wealthy. Congratulate yourself on becoming wealthy and hear others congratulating you as well. You should realize that although this might appear to be a game you are playing, you are doing one of the wisest things you can possibly do—you are working from a higher to a lower potential.

You are embarking on a program of self-development. You are about to learn that there is much more to your self than meets the eye, and you must apprehend this "hidden factor of your personality," if you are ever to develop yourself properly. In truth, you will never see the greatest part of your being because it is nonphysical in nature. In fact, you will soon become aware that you are constantly living simultaneously on three distinct planes of being: you are spiritual, you have an intellect and you live in a physical body.

To understand this abstraction better, you must keep in mind that you are living simultaneously on three distinct planes of existence.

1) The Spiritual Plane of Thoughts
   (Highest Potential)

2) The Intellectual Plane of Ideas
   (Middle Potential)

3) The Physical Plane of Results
   (Lowest Potential).

Therefore, by doing what I have suggested you do, you are merely using your "divine nature" to choose the thoughts (i.e. "Money is good," "I love people and I use money," "Money is a servant; I am the master,") which will build an idea. In our case, the idea happens to be that of "Great Personal Wealth," or "True Financial Success." Be very aware that ideas, such as the idea of "financial success," never form by themselves; the human personality must always enter into the process, by thinking the thoughts which can then be used to build the idea. That is the very thing that makes the human being "godlike," or you could say, a creative creature—the highest form of creation! So by holding this beautiful idea, or picture of financial success in your mind, you will ultimately be able to cause the idea to manifest itself in your life (i.e. in your results). As you progress through this book, you will see how this actually occurs!

Now, let's take a couple of steps backward. You will remember that I wrote, in a previous paragraph, that you are working from a higher to a lower potential. What I meant by this is that you are working from—

Thoughts ... (Spirit)
to
Idea ... (Intellectual)
to
Thing ... (Physical)

rather than working from—

Thing ... (Physical)
to
Thoughts ... (Spirit)
to
Idea ... (Intellectual)

as you have probably done in the past and as the vast majority of people will continue to do in the future. That is to say, most people will look at a result in their life and then let that result dictate the Thoughts they will then use to build their Idea. For example, if they see that their bank account is empty (a result), they will choose to think thoughts of lack or loss and then they will use those thoughts to build the idea of poverty. However, since the idea they are holding in their mind must manifest in their future results, they are actually bringing about a repeat performance of the very thing which they say they don't want: namely, an empty bank account. It thus becomes a self-doom-fulfilling cycle they are living, and clearly, this is not the way our Maker has intended for us to live!

You might very well be saying to yourself that this is an absurd argument; for if a bank account is empty, it's empty. It just isn't realistic to look at an empty bank account and be able to visualize great wealth. But I want you to know, this is the very kind of reasoning which perpetuates poverty and keeps poor people impoverished!

You must begin to understand that the present state of your bank account, your sales, your health, your social life, your position at work, etc., is nothing more than the physical manifestation of your previous thinking. If you sincerely wish to change or improve your results in your physical world, you must change your thoughts and you must change them immediately.

If you take the time to really think through the information which is being presented, you will conclude that what has just been said makes perfect sense. In fact, anyone who truly understands the "creative process," will tell you what I have just said is not only right, but it is a natural law of your being— it is the way God works with and through the individual. This is also called prayer in some "circles" ("prayer" being the movement that takes place between spirit and form, with and through the individual). God has given you the ability to build any idea which you desire. You were "Born Rich" and your abundance is contained in thought. So be good to yourself, choose magnificent ideas, and cease permitting your physical world to control your thinking.

You can readily understand, by now, how

everyone makes the "great mistake." In Emerson's essay on Self-Reliance he said, "Envy is ignorance." In other words, to look at another person's "Accomplishments," or "Results," and then to envy them, is truly unwise. For those people first chose their thoughts, in order to build the picture in their mind of the good that is now manifest in their life; and they chose those thoughts from the infinite source of supply which is available to all of us— you as well!

That is what the great artist, Vincent Van Gogh, meant when he was asked how he did such beautiful work. He said, "I dream my painting, and then I paint my dream." In other words, he saw the picture in his mind first and then he made a replica on canvas— in oil, of the original in his mind. In truth, there has never been an "original" "Van Gogh" sold! As I am writing this I can see you reading it, and can almost hear you thinking, "That makes a lot of sense—now I see."

A few years ago Mary Snyder from California sat in one of my seminars with her husband Oscar. She gave me a quote by Lincoln which I truly love and which I have shared with thousands of people. Lincoln said, "To believe in the things you can see and touch is no belief at all; but to believe in the unseen is a triumph and a blessing." Isn't that beautiful? Thanks again, Mary.

Hopefully by now you understand the wisdom of some of these mental exercises I have been suggesting. So keep repeating: "I am prosperous, I am wealthy, money is good." See yourself in your mind's eye, doing what you will do when you have the manifestation of your new attitude or consciousness. Visualize this great wealth and feel yourself already in possession of it. Remember though, money is the servant; you are the master— you love people and you use money.

Before you continue on to the next chapter, reread this chapter, "Me And Money," because rereading it will help you release that old idea about money, which causes an uncomfortable feeling whenever the subject of money is raised. Repeat to yourself, several times each day, "Me And Money," until you become totally aware of how good you feel thinking about wealth.

Refrain from talking to a lot of people about this new idea concerning money, until you have a firm grip on it yourself and feel confident about explaining what you have learned to others. Remember, hearing negative comments from people who do not understand the truth will not do you any good—if it does anything, it will only cause you to doubt yourself. You must not permit this to happen, because when you think about "Me And Money," you want a beautiful picture to fly onto the screen of your mind!

> *"The good life is expensive.*
> *There is another way to live*
> *that doesn't cost as much*
> *but it isn't any good".*
>
> Spanish Distillers

Chapter 2

HOW
MUCH IS
ENOUGH

HOW MUCH IS ENOUGH?

*"Most people think they want more money
than they really do,
and they settle for a lot less
than they could get."*
Earl Nightingale

For you to get this prosperity concept into high gear, you must be specific—exactly how much money do you want? Remember, you are working with your subconscious mind and the subconscious does not think. It merely accepts images and then moves them into form. So for you to say, I want "lotsa money" isn't good enough, because no one, least of all the subconscious mind, knows how much "lotsa" is.

I strongly recommend that you get very serious about this chapter, because the idea it contains could literally change your life. But understand that thinking, by itself, is not enough—you must move into action. There are certain things you must do and the first one is to decide how much money you want.

For you to answer this question, it would probably be a good idea for you to decide what you want the money for. But to simply say, "I want the money to live on," is not good enough. You should realize our society is structured in such a way that the government will "keep you." In fact, in most places, they will even mail a check to you—you can sit at home and still receive a "living wage."

At this point you are probably saying to yourself, "Oh yes, I know that, but I want to live better than that." Well, let's get specific—how much better? Bearing in mind that this kind of an exercise is going to require some serious planning on your part, get out a sheet of paper and draw up a list of all the "things," or "activities," that you plan to spend money on over the course of the next year. To assist you in getting started with your list, I have outlined several sample categories below:

Food, Rent/Mortgage, Clothes, Automobile, Utilities, Education, Vacations, Recreation, Insurance, Savings.

Understandably, these are just a few of the many possibilities; so keep working on your own list until it is complete! And remember, you do not fill in the amounts you are now spending. Rather, you take each item on the list, visualize how you want to live and then fill in the amount of money it will cost you to do so. For example, you might only go out to a nice restaurant to dine on very special occasions, but you might visualize yourself spending a very enjoyable evening out for dinner once a week, where the service is excellent, the food is even better, and the environment is fit for royalty. How much would that cost? — that is the figure you're looking for.

You could be driving a car that is getting old and is showing signs of rust, but you might visualize yourself driving a brand new car of your choice, that you trade every year or two. How much would that cost? Remember, you do not have a contract to live forever, nor is this a practice run—this is your life and you should be enjoying it to the fullest extent humanly possible! Therefore, you should have the amount of money you need, to provide the things you want, to live the way you choose to live.

Let me caution you—it would not be unusual for your mind to be playing tricks on you at this point. You could be thinking, "This is really crazy. I'm never going to have the money to live the way this book suggests." I want to remind you, however, that there are many people who do have enough money to live the way this book suggests—and they weren't born with it—and no one left it to them. They were "Born Rich" in the sense of having the God-given potential to succeed (everyone is), but like most people, they were at one time short of money. Understand that you too can succeed, and you will, if you will only do as this book suggests.

As I am writing this, I feel compelled to digress for a few lines, to remind you that you have great resources of talent and ability locked up, within you, just waiting to be expressed. In this vein, I can vividly recall listening to a tape a number of years ago, that Earl Nightingale made on "Attitude." I must have listened to that tape literally hundreds of times and there was a part on it where he said, "Now, right here we come to a rather strange fact. We tend to minimize the things we can do, the goals we can reach, and yet, for some equally strange reason, we think others can do things that we cannot." Earl went on to say, "I want you to know that that is not true. You do have deep reservoirs of talent and ability within you, and you can have the things you want."

I wouldn't even want to speculate on how many times I heard that section, without really understanding what he meant; and then one day I heard it, and every cell in my brain seemed to resonate with the truth of what he said. I suddenly realized what he was "driving at" and I knew deep down inside of me, if they can do it, so can I, if I am willing to pay the price. Please understand you too can do it, because what Earl had to say is as true of you as it was of me. But part of the price for you, is to figure out ...

How Much Is Enough?

Don't just pull a figure out of the sky. Do it right—because when you're finished you will be glad you did. Moreover, this exercise will also help you to develop a more disciplined mind. At this point you might be thinking this section doesn't even concern you, because you are already too deeply in debt to start accumulating a sizeable amount of money. But you will be happy to know, we have a great idea which will help you deal with that problem as well. Furthermore, you will be delighted to know that in many situations—and yours may be one of them—a person can become wealthy, even if he or she never earns any more money than they are earning currently. That thought alone should give you the encouragement you need to continue reading.

By now you should have completed your list and arrived at a figure; so take pen to paper and write that number down in big bold figures. Now, clear your mind of that idea and move on with me to another very important idea. Realize that although this idea might not apply specifically to you—at least at the present time—it certainly will apply to many readers. Moreover, even if it does not apply to your particular situation, it is worth thinking through anyway, because you certainly have many friends and associates it does apply to and you will be able to share it with them.

I am going to explain this idea to you as if you were a married person with a family to support and you are either the sole breadwinner or an important contributor.

Now one of the principal reasons for wanting the amount of money you desire is to provide for your family, and not just in an adequate manner. After all, you want them to live life to its fullest. Realize, therefore, that as long as you live and are able to follow the plan outlined in this book, you will be able to do as you want with respect to your family. However, if you really stop and think about it, you will very likely agree that you would want your family to live "the good life," even if you were suddenly removed from the picture—wouldn't you? Jokingly you might say, "No, who cares if I'm gone." But this is not a joking matter. This is a very serious matter. Of course you care—I know it and so do you!

Now, if you're alive and healthy, you will create this wealth for your estate. But what if you die or are permanently disabled? Well, our society has taken care of that situation as well; we have "Life Insurance" and we have "Disability Insurance."

But, let's get back to your thinking again—you might be saying to yourself, "Life insurance, what a rip-off. This guy Bob Proctor really doesn't know where he is coming from." Well, let me tell you, that when it comes to life insurance, I believe I can claim to be an authority of sorts—for I have conducted seminars for the insurance industry for almost ten years, and I have had close to 50,000 people from that industry "go through" my seminars. Therefore, I can assure you, that when I say approximately 95% of the people whom you talk to are almost completely ignorant when it comes to the subject of insurance, I am not "talking through my hat." Granted, many of these people hold important positions in business and industry, in government, or in the professions, and because of their positions, it would be very easy to just assume they know "of whence they speak." But the sad fact of the matter is, many of them are either badly misinformed or completely uninformed when it comes to the important subject of life insurance.

Understand this—there is no way to replace your income and create a certain and instant estate other than life insurance; and statistics indicate that although most people are insured, the vast majority of people (at least 90%), are dangerously under-insured. That is to say, when they die, most people leave behind only enough money to pay for their funeral and possibly enough money to cover their family's living expenses for one year! The unfortunate part is, that for a relatively small sum of money, these people could have had their financial affairs set up in such a way that if something did happen to them, their financial goals would be reached by their families automatically.

Since this book is designed to help you reach a substantial, financial goal, I felt duty-bound to include the information on life insurance. The book could not be complete without it.

(Keep in mind there are only two ways to earn money: people at work, or money at work.)

You will be happy to know the remainder of this book is designed for the person who is going to LIVE,.

Bloom Where You Are Planted—Start Now!

When do you start to live this good life? Is that the question you are beginning to ask yourself? You start now.

Start by answering the following questions:

How often do you pay your phone bill?
How often do you pay your rent or mortgage?
How often do you pay your grocery store?
How often do you pay for gas for your car?
How often do you pay your doctor?
How often do you pay yourself?

That last question seems like a strange one, doesn't it? But do you realize that less than 5 people in every 100 ever pay themselves. And, if you were to ask the other 95 why they don't, they would probably tell you that by the time they pay everyone else, there is nothing left for themselves!

Clearly, those 4 or 5 people in every 100 who do "pay themselves," have found a way around this problem. Although the idea which they are employing has been around for centuries, hardly anyone today is aware of it. What is that idea, you ask? Simply put it is this:

"They pay themselves FIRST!"

(This is better known as the Babylonian law of financial success.)

A Part Of All You Earn Is Yours To Keep

If you think about it, you must admit this "law," or principle, makes a lot of good sense. Therefore, let me repeat it - "A part of all you earn is yours to keep!" More specifically, what you earn Monday morning is yours to keep, so it should go directly into a special account that you do not have easy access to.

Your Financial Independence Account

What you earn on Monday morning probably represents ten percent of your income. Therefore, you should pay yourself at least that ten percent, right off the top (i.e. not after everyone else has been paid).

From your "Financial Independence Account," you first pay your insurance premium, because that instrument creates your "Instant Estate." The remainder of the money then goes into savings, until such time as you have accumulated enough capital to make a wise investment. Remember, you do not "touch" this account or the interest it will yield. Therefore, within a very short period of time, you will witness sufficient progress to gain the motivation and inspiration which you need to continue. Moreover, the knowledge that you have an "Instant Estate," if anything should happen to you, will give you additional serenity of mind.

Orderly Debt Repayment Program

You could already have debts that seem to be eating up your entire paycheck, leaving nothing for yourself. But understand this—these debts can be retired. (Although the amount of debt you have incurred will, of course, determine the length of time it will take you to clear the slate.) And, for the purposes of the following discussion, you must consider your mortgage or house payment (probably one of your largest monthly payments), as an investment, NOT a debt.

Debt Clearance Account

Whatever money you earn Monday afternoon and Tuesday morning, should go directly into your Debt Clearance Account. This represents twenty percent of your income. You should also sit down and draft a letter which you will send to all of your creditors, advising them of your plan.

However, before you mail the letter, you should first draw up a list of your creditors to determine what proportion of this twenty percent each of them would receive. It could conceivably be more money than they are presently receiving, or it could be less; but whichever way it works out, that will be the sum of money they will each receive. Nevertheless, whatever sum they do receive, they will receive it regularly, on the stipulated dates.

The following is a sample letter you could use as a guide in drafting your own letter:

Dear Whomever:

As you know, I am in debt to you for $_____, and I intend to pay you in full, plus interest. In order to achieve this goal, I have been devising a plan during the past few days to put myself in a stable financial position. To this end, I have opened a "Debt Clearance Account" (DCA), and twenty percent of my income is going directly into that account. That will enable me to have sufficient resources to live on, without worry or stress, and it will prevent me from falling further into debt.

Each week (or month) you will receive a check for $_____ from my "DCA," until my account with you is clear. I am aware that this is not the figure I had previously agreed to pay you, but I'm sure you will be understanding, and appreciate what I am doing.

If you have any questions, please feel free to contact me. I am quite excited about my new plans and if you would like to have me review them with you so that you might help others who are in your debt, I would be pleased to do so.

Thank you in advance for your kind cooperation.

Have a wonderful day!

Sincerely

John Doe

Understand that your letter to your creditor is a statement of fact and not a request—it is you who is in charge of your finances, not your creditors!

Be sure to have your letters neatly typed and enclose your first new payment with your covering letter. Realize there is an "outside chance" that some unreasonable person will not want to cooperate with you. They might even go so far as to phone you and attempt to intimidate you with threats of taking you to court, etc. But please hold your ground, because there is no court in the country that would not congratulate you, when you explained your entire plan for Financial Independence. Moreover, you will find that 95% of the people, to whom you write, will be most cooperative.

Now give yourself a good "pat on the back," because as of this moment, you are well on your way to starting a completely new way of life!

Let's briefly review what you have accomplished thus far:

1)   You have an instant estate if anything should happen to you.

2)   You have a savings account.

3)   You are paying yourself.

4)   You have an orderly debt repayment program.

5)   You have 70% of your income to live on; to run the house and for entertainment.

6)   Your mind is clear to carry on with the big ideas coming your way in the remainder of this book.

From this moment on, never think "debt" again. Remember, that has all been taken care of—so just focus on your savings account, and watch it grow. Repeat—I am wealthy; Money is good; I use money and I love people.

Metaphorically speaking, getting your present finances in order is very similar to having your automobile tuned up for a journey which you are about to take. Realize that as of this moment, you are tuned up for your journey. And, although you might only be earning "x" number of dollars per year presently, you must see yourself, on the screen of your mind, already earning the new annual income which you have calculated you need, to buy the things you want, in order to live the way you choose to live.

If you are seriously interested in becoming financially independent and you have not yet acted on the preceding ideas, I would strongly recommend you do so now. For to continue on to the next chapter, without having done so, would be comparable to leaving on your journey with your car firing on only half its cylinders. You can be almost certain that your automobile will break down, preventing you from reaching your desired destination. But by making certain that everything is properly "tuned up," you can relax and adopt a calm, serene attitude, knowing that you will get to your destination; and you will certainly be able to enjoy the scenery along the way!

If you find that the task of getting your financial world in good order for this exciting journey is something which you are not able to do alone, I would strongly suggest you seek out professional assistance. (This is something that almost all wealthy people do.) That is to say, wealthy individuals follow the advice of financial experts. It is similar in principle to the idea that if a person's body were sick, he or she would likely seek out a skilled physician for advice. Moreover, you should also keep in mind that even healthy people, if they are wise, periodically go to a doctor for a checkup. In other words, you do not always need to get sick in order to get better.

It has already been brought to your attention that very few people ever develop real expertise in the area of serious "financial planning."

Therefore, you should seek out a competent financial counselor, in much the same manner as you would seek assistance, in matters of a legal nature. There are companies that provide this type of financial service in every city. In some places they are not too easy to find; but they are there, if you will only look for them.

I had the pleasure of being instrumental in the

start-up of just such a company, in the city of Toronto, Canada in 1979 (the name of the company is The McCrary Group). Today the company has almost five thousand happy clients, who are well on their way to financial independence. The McCrary Group makes all of its clients very aware of an interesting financial fact, which I would like to share with you at this time.

This fact is, people fall into three distinct categories with respect to "finances":

1.   Deficit position (in debt),
2.   Break-even position (just getting by, but debt-free),
3.   Surplus position.

It would be very easy to "trick" oneself into believing, that if one were in category one or two, all one must do is earn more money, and then one would automatically graduate into the third category. But of course, this is not necessarily true. For if a person is in a deficit financial position, it means they are in the "habit" of spending more money than they earn. Similarly, if they are in a break-even position, they are in the habit of spending everything they earn. Since we are all "creatures of habit," it follows that earning more money would not necessarily change our overall financial position. It is vitally important, that when you decide "how much is enough," you also design a new financial plan or have one designed for you which will force you to discipline yourself—at least for a month or two—until you form the new habit of living by that new plan.

The next chapter, "The Image Maker," will help you to understand how and why you must begin to see yourself already earning that new figure. But for the time being, just bear in mind that as your income increases, the ten percent you are saving increases and the twenty percent that is going into your DCA increases, which means that you will be able to retire your debts faster. Furthermore, you will then be left with 90% of your income on which to live. (I can see you getting excited about this idea already!)

Chapter 3

THE IMAGE-MAKER

It's Up To Me

I get discouraged now and then
When there are clouds of gray,
Until I think about the things
That happened yesterday.
I do not mean the day before
Or those of months ago,
But all the yesterdays in which
I had the chance to grow.
I think of opportunities
That I allowed to die,
And those I took advantage of
Before they passed me by.
And I remember that the past
Presented quite a plight,
But somehow I endured it and
The future seemed all right.
And I remind myself that I
Am capable and free,
And my success and happiness
Are really up to me.

James J. Metcalfe

THE IMAGE-MAKER

The ideas contained in this chapter could very well be the breakthrough for you, because Image-Making, once we get a firm grip on it, is a truly dynamic idea.

I was speaking in Ohio a number of years ago, to a large group of business people, when an elderly gentleman in the audience suddenly stopped me as I was explaining the Image-Making concept. He stood up and informed the audience that he was sixty-five years of age, before he understood this idea. He mentioned that he had read about it, thought about it, and even talked about it, but he never really understood it until he was sixty-five years old.

I want to suggest, right at this moment, that you read this chapter over a few times, because most people live and die and never fully understand the power of Image-Making. Understand that we are relating this idea to "money" in this book; but I want you to know that once you fully understand the Image-Making concept, you can effectively use it for whatever good you desire.

I am not able to tell you the exact date on which I myself gained an understanding of Image-Making, but I can tell you it has had as great an impact on my life as any idea I have ever learned.

The knowledge of Image-Making eliminates competition from your life, by moving you from the competitive plane to the creative plane. You will soon understand therefore, that in truth, the only competition you will ever have is with your own ignorance.

This idea truly excites me. To be more accurate, I should probably say sharing this idea with you excites me, because I know how it can improve every aspect of your life. I honestly love watching people grow or unfold as new ideas register in their consciousness.

But before I delve into this idea, please understand that everyone is using the Image-Making concept and everyone always has. In fact, everything that has ever come into your life has come as a direct result of the Image-Making process. Therefore, if you will only become aware of the results which you have obtained, you will realize you have already employed this great mental tool. Just take a look at the results most people obtain. Generally speaking, you could say it is quite obvious that when they make use of their Image-Making ability, they almost always use it the wrong way.

You Are An Image-Maker

Most religions teach that God is responsible for everything made in this world and I would fully subscribe to this proposition. However, as co-creators, human beings must bear responsibility for WHAT God makes in their lives.

The Minister And The Farmer

A story I once heard illustrates this point

exceedingly well. Many years ago, a minister was driving along a remote country road, when he happened upon a very beautiful farm. The farm was kept in absolutely magnificent condition. The fences were well cared for, the crops were a radiant green and although the house was set back some distance from the road, it was abundantly clear that it had a clean, fresh coat of white paint on it. Well-cultivated flower beds encircled the house and stretched all along both sides of the long, wide driveway, leading to it from the road. In a neat row along both sides of the drive as well, were straight lines of tall green poplar trees reaching up to a picturesque pale blue sky. The lawns surrounding the house were a deep rich green, and as well manicured as any putting green ever was. Indeed, the entire picture would have fit well on a post card, since it was absolutely breathtaking in its splendor.

Then the minister looked off to his right, to the other side of the road. Here the fields were ploughed, the earth was the deepest black the minister had ever seen and he was amazed at how the furrows had been plowed in such a way that they stretched out in rows "as straight as clothes lines." Far off in the distance, the minister could see the farmer sitting up on his tractor, with a straw hat on the back of his head and clad in an old, light blue pair of overalls. It appeared that the farmer was moving toward the road as he was plowing. Since the minister was in no particular hurry, he pulled his car over to the side of the road, got out of it, and walked toward the fence. When he reached it, he just stood still, enjoying the light breeze, the warm sunlight and admiring the beauty of the farm and the farmer's ability to plough such straight furrows.

As the farmer worked his way toward the road, he noticed the minister leaning against the fence. So he brought the tractor to a halt, climbed down from it, and slowly started to walk in the minister's direction. As the farmer got closer the minister smiled, raised his arm, and waved saying, "My good man, God has certainly blessed you with a beautiful farm."

The farmer stopped, pulled out an old red and white polka-dot handkerchief from his pocket with his big, scarred and calloused hands. He raised his arm and wiped the sweat from his sun-scorched brow, still not saying a word. Then he reached up with his other hand, and gently took from his mouth the long piece of straw that had been bouncing and waving as he walked.

He stood in silence for a moment, looking at the minister, and then he spoke. With a slow, steady voice be replied, "Yes Reverend, you're right. God has blessed me with a beautiful farm, but I just wish you could have seen it when he had it all to himself!"

Understand that "images" are mental pictures that are made from thoughts, and the magnificence of the mind lies in the fact that it can "think." That is to say, it can tap into thought and create whatever image it chooses.

Now play with your mind for a few minutes and become aware of how you can flash one picture or image after another on the screen of your mind. It is almost as if you were sitting inside your body at a great theatre, and you are the writer, producer and director of this movie you are watching.

In a wonderful book I read a number of years ago titled The Science of Getting Rich, the author, Wallace D. Wattles, referred to "This thinking stuff that permeates, penetrates, and fills the interspaces of the cosmos." It's true that thoughts are everywhere and we can tap into this thinking stuff with our mind and form any image we choose.

Now become aware of this truth. Everything we do is preceded by an image. We think first in order to form an image, then we do the work.

Building The First Chair

Consider for a moment how the first "chair" was built. We did not always have chairs, you know. I suppose many years ago when we first started to become civilized, someone became tired of sitting on the ground. Whoever this person was, he probably started to think, and began to see a picture in his mind. He probably saw himself sitting on a "thing" with his legs hanging down and his back leaning against something. This picture or idea appealed to him, because he imagined that it would be a more comfortable position in which to sit; certainly much more comfortable than sitting on the ground with his knees shoved up under his chin!

Since this picture appealed to the person, the person thought of it often, until a desire to have such a thing began to develop. The desire moved the person into action, and with the picture in his mind, he began to build something outside of himself—in his physical world—that was, as close as possible, a replica of the image he held in his mind. Once the thing was completed, the person sat on it. He let his legs hang and his back lean and he found that it was good. He then called the thing a "chair." The word "chair" is a symbol that has a corresponding image and when you see or hear the symbol chair, it triggers an image on the screen of your mind. From that day to this, others have been building images of more comfortable chairs—chairs with padding, chairs that fold and chairs that recline. Then someone got lonely sitting alone and the person began to think and they built an image in their mind of a very long chair. They constructed that long chair, found it was good and they called it a "sofa."

Need we continue? Someone got tired of sleeping under a tree and they built an image of a roof over their head and on and on we go. Out of the cave into a condominium. We have truly built the world we live in.

Columbus imaged a new world and you and I are living in it. The Wright Brothers imaged us being propelled through the air and introduced us to a new kingdom. Samuel Morse imaged himself interrupting the flow of energy through metallic wires and gave us the telegraph with the Morse code. Copernicus imaged a multiplicity of worlds and now we have been there.

Through the years, history has recorded the results of great visionaries. In fact, everything ever accomplished was at first, and for a time, nothing more than an image held in the mind of the architect. Realize, now, that you too are the "mental architect" of your own destiny.

Going To The Movies

Consider this: Jack Nicklaus, the world famous golfer, explains he will not even pick up a club until he has a very clear image on the screen of his mind, showing exactly how the ball will fly through the air, how it will hit the ground and where it will roll after it hits. Nicklaus calls this "going to the movies" and he has become so proficient at it that he has become known throughout the world. Fame and fortune are his for the asking.

In a previous paragraph, I made reference to the statement by Wallace D. Wattles: "There is a thought stuff that permeates, penetrates and fills the interspaces of the cosmos." In truth, there is a thought stuff everywhere around you and within you. So become aware of this truth and tap into it now. Use it to form an image on the screen of your mind; see yourself already in possession of the amount of money you want, to provide the things you need, to live in the style you choose to live.

Personal Prosperity

You are using mental faculties that everyone has. They are exactly the same mental faculties used by Copernicus, Buddha and Morse whom we previously mentioned. You might have formed the habit of thinking that people like those just mentioned are different than you and I. But I want you to know the only difference between you and them, or anyone else, is only in appearance and accomplishments. We all live in different physical bodies and we all use our inherent mental faculties in a different way; but our basic structure is fundamentally the same.

I am well aware there are many professors and other professional people who will tell you what I have just said is a lot of nonsense. But disbelievers like these have always existed and they are, in my opinion, little people. For all of the truly great leaders are in complete agreement with what I have just explained, about your equality with great people of the past and present.

Even Jesus tried to tell the world, as he was doing his great work some two thousand years ago, that you too were capable of doing what he was doing. In fact, He even went a step further in saying, "Even greater things are you capable of." Believe Him, He spoke the truth. The little people will say, that is not what He meant. But let me assure you, it is exactly what Jesus meant. If you can see it and believe it—you can do it.

Napoleon Hill spent almost his entire life studying five hundred of the world's greatest achievers and the essence of his exhaustive studies and writings is contained in his great book, Think and Grow Rich. "Whatever the mind can conceive and believe it can achieve." Not many people believe this, but the ones who do, prove it to themselves. Why don't you prove it to yourself, now.

Just build the image of prosperity on the screen of your mind and watch what happens. Remember though, regardless of how tough things get, you must continue to hold the picture of personal prosperity. You will very likely run up against a series of circumstances that will, for a time, almost have you convinced you are actually going backwards; but, persistence is the key. Continue to hold the picture of personal prosperity and understand that what is happening to you, is what must happen, to prepare you to receive the good you desire.

"Persistence"—Napoleon Hill devoted an entire chapter in Think and Grow Rich to persistence. In that chapter he said, "There may be no heroic connotation to the word persistence, but the character is to the quality of man what carbon is to steel." Hill also pointed out in another part of the same chapter, that the only thing which separated Thomas Edison or Henry Ford from the rest of the people in the world was persistence. For both of these great men had an image and they would not let anyone or anything dissuade them—they were persistent. One illuminated the world, the other put the world on wheels. Both were, of course, richly rewarded.

In a previous chapter, we explained money is a reward for service rendered. These men provided a tremendous service to millions of individuals and their reward was in direct proportion to the service rendered. So build your image of prosperity and be persistent. The way for your image to materialize will be shown to you.

Persistence Always Pays

A number of years ago, John Kanary, a friend and business partner of mine, was discussing Hill's chapter on "persistence" with me. We both seemed to be equally impressed with the importance of this quality, as well as with the necessity of a person having it, if they were to reach any worthwhile goal. After a time and nearing the end of our discussion, we each agreed we would read the chapter on "persistence", once every day for thirty days. I don't even have to ask John to find out if this exercise helped him—I know it did; and the exercise has most certainly benefited me on numerous occasions.

There is an interesting story concerning John Kanary, which would be very appropriate to share with you here, since it illustrates both the power of "imaging," as well as "persistence."

Although I had known John Kanary for a couple of years and had talked with him on many occasions, I certainly did not know him as intimately as I do at the time of this writing. It is important that I bring this out here, as I will be referring back to it shortly. The incident I am about to relate, took place in 1971.

I was living in Chicago at the time and had just completed a speaking engagement in Edmonton, Alberta. When I returned to my room, there was a telephone message for me to call John Kanary, in Belleville, Ontario, Canada. I returned the call and after a couple of minutes of small talk, John said it was rather important that he meet with me, as he had something he wanted to discuss and he preferred not to "go into it" on the telephone. I asked John to wait while I looked over my calendar; it was, in the vernacular—packed tight. I was busy, to say the least; almost every day I had either a seminar or speaking engagement in a different city in North America. I explained this to John and told him that although I would love to visit, I really didn't know when I could. John was persistent, so I said, "Listen, I'm leaving Edmonton for Chicago tonight at midnight. To get to Chicago I have to go through Toronto. I'll arrive there at 7 a.m. I'll have to change terminals and I leave from the second terminal, one hour and fifty minutes later. I'll be happy to talk to you then, although I don't promise to be too alert after flying all night."

It is also worth mentioning that John had to get up early enough to drive the 125 miles from Belleville to Toronto, to meet my 7:00 a.m. arrival. I remember that all John said was, "I'll be there."

The next morning I sat in the airport coffee shop and listened as John explained how he "wanted to do what I was doing." He wanted to conduct seminars. He also explained that he was prepared to pay the price, whatever it might be.

As I listened, it was like hearing a popular song on the radio—you keep hearing it, over and over again. In almost every seminar I conduct there is a man or woman in the seminar who wants to do "what I am doing." I've heard it in Biloxi, Mississippi; Butte, Montana; Los Angeles, New York, Moncton and Montreal—it was an old tune. Now, here I was in Toronto with a friend who, as I have already mentioned, I did not know that well, and he was asking what "he had to do."

As I was listening, the same images, which I had with all the others, were flashing through my mind. I was remembering all the travelling and the fear of standing up and speaking in a large hotel ballroom crowded with people who wanted you to get them excited, but who were mentally putting you on trial at the same time, thinking, "Does this guy know what he is talking about?" In many situations, such as a sales convention, you had forty minutes from beginning to end in which to build rapport with a few hundred strangers and get them excited about themselves.

The years of staying up nights reading and studying, the years of learning by attending seminars all over the continent, the years of working for next to nothing to prepare oneself to hold the attention of a group of people all day in a seminar, these were the images racing across my mind. It had taken me eleven years to get to that point.

But how do you say, "No, you'll never do it," when someone like John asks you, especially when the essence of what you teach is —you can do anything. Yet, how can you say "yes," when everyone you know, with the exception of two or three others besides yourself, cannot earn a living in the public speaking business unless they are a celebrity. (And that is a whole different story.)

When John Kanary finished, I told him what I had told all the others: "Yes, you can do it, but it's tough. Make sure you understand that, John. It's tough. You will have to do a tremendous amount of studying, because you not only have to know what to say, but you must also have the answers to a thousand and one questions arising as a result of what you say. Some of the questions will come from professional people—medical doctors, engineers and lawyers—who, in most cases, know what they are talking about. So you not only have to be right, but confident as well, or you will be discredited with your entire audience; and that only has to happen a couple of times and you're "out of business."

You not only have to study these ideas, but you must use them as well, or there will be no conviction in your talks. (Not to mention the fact that you will be a walking physical contradiction to what you teach.) It is next to impossible, for example, to have a sick person teaching 'health'.

You must develop showmanship and voice control, and on and on it goes. In short, John, for every one who makes it, a thousand fail miserably."

Usually when this is explained, the person says they still want to go ahead, but you never hear from them again. John was no exception, in one sense— he still wanted to go ahead. However, in every other way he was an exception. I did see him again. I told him what to read and what to do and he read it and did it. John read hundreds of books—he "devoured" them. He narrated them onto tapes and then played the tapes in the car. At his own expense, he followed me all over the country and sat in hundreds of seminars. He wrote thousands of pages of notes and studied them diligently.

Finally, I would have him open and close the seminars. Then he would conduct part of a seminar himself. In the beginning he was full of fear, he was soaking wet. Sometimes he would be so worried about what the audience thought of him, that he would forget everything he knew and, as you know, an audience can be very cruel. But despite all this he continued. (Keep in mind this was costing him money; he was not being paid.)

John Kanary had built an image of himself doing "what I was doing" and he would not quit. He was persistent and it worked. It always has and it always will. Today he has earned the respect of many of the world's largest corporations. He has spoken in almost every major city in North America. He has also earned more in one day than he was earning in a year when I first met him!

So if someone with numerous degrees after their name tells you Image-Making and Persistence don't work, just look John Kanary up and ask him. He will tell you, "I know you can do it, because I did it!"

Philip Nacola, a minister in Santa Anna, California, preached a sermon on a similar idea one Sunday, that I was fortunate enough to hear when I was living there. He said, "Keep your mind on a higher image rather than a lower concern." I realize that is not always an easy thing to do, but it sure pays great dividends for the person who develops the mental strength to do it, and that is what it takes—mental strength.

Build your image now and develop the mental strength to hold it.

A number of years ago, prior to Napoleon Hill's death, Earl Nightingale condensed and narrated Think and Grow Rich onto a long playing record. At the end of the record Mr. Hill comes on to close the record. He said, "And now as I stretch out the hand of friendship through time and space, let me remind you, not to go searching for opportunity in the distance, but reach out and embrace it right where you are."

Wattles said, "This thinking stuff, permeates and penetrates the entire universe." They are both telling us the same thing. So build your image now, right where you are. Don't even wait until you finish this book. Build it now and let the remaining pages in this book strengthen the image. You don't even have to try, just let the image of a more prosperous you float to the center of your consciousness. It's already here, so let it appear.

For many years now, I have been very aware of the power that flows through you to accomplish good in your life, when you hold the proper image in your mind; and this great truth has been responsible for many wonderful things happening in my own life. Moreover, I have also seen numerous examples of what a proper image will do in the lives of other people.

Paul Hutsey's Story

I would be remiss if I concluded this chapter without sharing Paul Hutsey's story with you. It all began when I received a telephone call from Charlie Beck, who was the Vice President of Sales for the southwestern Home Office of the Prudential Insurance Company of America, in Houston, Texas. He invited me to speak at the company's Regional Business Conferences, to be held in Toronto, Canada. He explained they had four different regions and each region was coming in for three days to the conference. (This meant that they wanted me to work in Toronto for approximately 12 days.) Although I was living in Los Angeles at the time, Toronto was my home town—where I grew up. My family and friends all lived there, so naturally the idea appealed to me. But I asked Charlie how long I could have on the program and he said, "about an hour." I think it is worth mentioning, at this point, that I have not as yet learned to teach anyone much in an hour, and I told him so. I explained that if he would give me two mornings on the program—with each region— I would be glad to come and do the job for him. I wanted two and one-half hours each morning.

Charlie's southern accent was interrupted by a real deep belly laugh as he explained that they had never done anything like that, in the 100 year history of the company. All of their executives had to take part in the program and so they never gave anyone that much time. However, I stood firm. I gave him the name of a couple of other vice-presidents in his company whom I had worked for and I suggested that he call them, to find out if my idea had any merit. But as I hung up the phone, I did so rather reluctantly because I really wanted the job. I must admit that I was somewhat surprised, therefore, when one of Charlie's aides phoned me back to say they were "going for it." He also told me he didn't know how I had talked Charlie into doing it, but I was given two mornings on the program. I made up my mind right on the spot that I was going to leave these people with something special—and if they chose to use it—they could literally change their lives overnight. (Not to mention what it would do for their sales records.) I was going to speak on the power of an image or, to be more specific, the power of a self-image and the benefits of holding a positive one.

At the conclusion of the program for one of the regions, a gentleman came up to me and said it was imperative he talk to me. He said he had a problem, and he felt I had the answer to the problem, because he was impressed with the ideas I had explained during the seminar presentations. There were approximately 200 people in each one of these conventions and I explained to this man that many of the people wanted to talk to me, but I did not have the time to talk to everyone individually, since I was only one person. I also explained to him I had another appointment and had to leave immediately to be there on time. Still, he was persistent, so I agreed to meet him the following morning in the coffee-shop for breakfast.

I can remember our meeting as if it were yesterday. The two of us sat down, just inside the door of the coffee-shop at the Hyatt House Hotel on

Avenue Road. As soon as we sat down, he started talking. He informed me that he had to tell me something about himself, so I could understand his problem. He said he did not want me to think he was bragging, but it was necessary for me to have this information.

He began by telling me he was a "good man," and I already knew that about him, just by looking at him. I could "feel" it about him. He then went on to explain he had worked for Prudential for more than 20 years, had been in management for all but two of those years, and he concluded by saying, "I'm a good manager." Next he stated he had a good record, good people, and he was well-respected by the executive staff of this company. No sooner had he uttered those words than Charlie Beck and Dick Merrill, the Senior Vice-President from Houston, came walking in. They came over to our table, congratulated Paul on his year, exchanged a few words with us and then went to their own table. Paul and I sat down again and resumed our conversation. He said, "They meant what they said." I knew it was true; it wasn't mere flattery. It was a sincere, merited compliment that Paul had received from his two senior executives. Finally, he said, "Now, this is my problem.

I run a district office in Wichita, Kansas. Out of over 500 offices Prudential has, our office stands in 175th place. Now," he said, "that's not bad, nothing to be ashamed of." And it wasn't—it was a fairly good standing. He then said, "My problem is, I know we are good enough to be in the top 100, and we're not. Every year I go for it, but I never seem to make it." At that moment I knew what the cause of Paul Hutsey's problem was. I explained to him that he was letting the sales sheet dictate the image he was holding in his mind. He saw himself as being number 175, and he was doing his utmost to move into the top 100. He worked hard, he worked with his people and, as he explained previously, he had good people. I showed Paul that it was imperative he see himself in the top 100, regardless of what the sales sheet said. In other words, he had to act as if he were already in the top 100. He had to become mentally what he wanted to be on the physical plane. He also had to learn how to communicate this idea to his entire staff.

Suddenly, I started to see the lights go on in Paul's mind. We talked for awhile longer, and I explained as much as I could about the mind to him—how it worked and especially about the power of holding the proper image there. Paul thanked me for the time I had given him and returned to Wichita, Kansas. As his region moved out of the Hyatt House, another one moved in. But about a day or so later, I received a long-distance call from Wichita, Kansas, and it was from Paul Hutsey. He wanted to know where I would be holding seminars when the conferences were completed. I told him I would be in southern Illinois for Prudential's mid-western home office. He then asked if he could join me and travel with me for two or three days. I explained to Paul that I had already made a deal with Charlie Beck to do our entire series of seminars for the whole of the southwestern home office, and one of the sites chosen was Paul's town—Wichita, Kansas.

Nevertheless, since we weren't going to be there for at least six weeks, he explained that he wanted to join me immediately. So, at his own expense, he flew some 600 miles to spend three days with me. We went together from Lichfield, Illinois, to LaSalle, Illinois. We spent hours talking as we were driving from one city to another, and he sat in the seminar and took copious notes, all day long. In the evening we would spend more hours conversing.

Finally, Paul returned to Wichita and started to apply these ideas. Specifically, he started to work with the proper image and, as a result, the sales started to climb. For some strange reason Paul's superiors saw fit to move him from Wichita, where he had been for a number of years, to Pittsburgh, Kansas, where the district office stood in 163rd position. This certainly didn't seem like a very fitting reward for all the effort he had advanced on the Company's behalf. Still, Paul accepted the move as a challenge, and a mere six months later the district in Pittsburgh, Kansas, stood number 11 in the entire Prudential Insurance Company!

Each year, Prudential recognizes the top fifty-two districts, which is the top 10%, by awarding them a citation. The Pittsburgh district had not had a citation in nine years. But just a short six months after Paul Hutsey took over the helm, they were in the top 2%. Just two years later, they missed the number one spot by a matter of a few percentage points. Today, Paul Hutsey is Vice-President of Sales in Houston, Texas, for the southwestern territory. Clearly, he is a man who learned well the awesome power of an image held in the mind. If you were to talk to Paul Hutsey today, he would be quick to tell you that he will never let present results dictate the image that he holds in his mind. Rather, he holds the image of what he wants and then acts as if he already has it.

Paul Hutsey is, without question, one of the best examples you will ever find when it comes to the subject of "building an image in the mind" and then executing it. He has become a serious student of the mind, and I am happy to count him among my good friends.

Understand this—you could be doing precisely what Paul Hutsey had been doing all those years. So if you are, then make up your mind right now to do what I have suggested you start doing. Start right where you are—build the image of what you want and then act as if you have already received it. Expressed somewhat differently, "Act like the person you want to become." For as Goethe, the German philosopher, once wrote, "Before you can do something, you first must be something."

As you finish this chapter, lay the book down and then become very relaxed. Let creative energy fill your consciousness and then mould it into an image of yourself in a much more abundant state of life. See yourself already in possession of what you previously only dreamed of. Become extremely conscious of the truth that your entire being is not only filled with, but also is surrounded by, the original substance all images are made of. So do not just keep reading page after page of the book without acting on the "suggestions" which I have been giving you.

In the introduction to this book, and then again in the first chapter, we emphasized the fact that, no amount of reading or memorizing will make you successful in life. It is the understanding and application of wise thought which counts. Understanding and application are the keys which will unlock the door to a truly abundant life.

It would be very tempting for you to flip from one page or idea to the next, thinking, "I know this, I know that." However, let me remind you, it makes no difference how accurately you can parrot back these concepts. In fact, you might even be able to recite them verbatim. Nevertheless, if you are not witnessing the results in your own life of the good you desire, you simply do not understand the power—and in fact the necessity—of acting on these ideas. Therefore, make the time right now, this very minute, to build the image in your mind of yourself already in possession of prosperity. Write a brief description of your image on a card, carry it in your pocket and read it every day, a number of times, until the image fills your consciousness.

Begin your written statement with:

I am so happy. I now see myself with

_____

_____

_____

_____

_____

_____

_____

_____

_____

_____

_____

_____

_____

_____

_____

_____

_____

_____

_____

_____

_____

Be good to yourself.
Treat yourself to the very best
life has to offer. Remember, quality is not
expensive, it's priceless!

Chapter 4

LET GO
AND
LET GOD

The Promised Land

No more shall I look to the far skies
for my Father's loving aid;
Since here upon earth His treasure lies,
and here is His kingdom laid.
No more through the mist of things unknown
I'll search for the Promised Land;
For time is the footstool of His throne,
and I am within His hand.

The wealth that is more than finest gold
is here,
if I shall but ask;
And wisdom unguessed and power untole
are here for every task.
The gates of heaven are before my eyes;
Their key is within my hand;
No more shall I look to the far skies;
For here is the Promised Land.

Alva Romanes

LET GO AND LET GOD

"Something wonderful is happening."
John Kanary
The Personal Coach

How many times have you been faced with what appeared to be an insurmountable problem and you silently wished you could "turn it over" to somebody else for a solution. Or have you ever sat day dreaming—building magnificent images on the screen of your mind—wishing you had a certain sum of money, wanting to take a trip to some exotic place, or possibly hoping to be able to purchase the automobile you have always wanted? Wouldn't it be fantastic if there was some "magic formula" that would give us the things we want and permit us to live the way we choose? Well there is, and it has been around since time began. Therefore, you can have the things you want—all of them—and you will have them if you will only make the ideas in this book a part of your way of thinking; a part of your way of life.

Make up your mind to read this chapter over and over—100 times if necessary—until you feel deep inside that you really comprehend the idea being expressed. For if you fail to grasp the idea presented to you in this chapter, the rest of the book will be of little value to you. However, once you do understand this chapter, it will be as if a tremendous light has gone on in your mind—truly illuminating your life— and you will realize you will never again be the same person you once were. No person, thing, or circumstance will intimidate you ever again. Your days of idle-wishing will be brought to a halt. Happiness, health and prosperity will follow you all the days of your life and you will spend the rest of your years wanting to share your new understanding with everyone and anyone who is willing to take the time to listen and learn.

Be aware, however, that many of the people whom you try to share your new awareness with are simply not ready for it. In fact, nine out of ten people will laugh and tell others you are odd, when you have shared your formula—Let Go And Let God— with them. You must realize this is because the vast majority of people whom you encounter every day, treat God like some cosmic bellboy, who is supposed to run and fetch and then deliver. These individuals erroneously believe that merely because a person verbalizes certain thoughts in their mind—"God please get me this," or "God give me that,"— they will receive what they have asked for. But unfortunately, these people do not understand the true nature of prayer and what is even more tragic— they don't even know, that they don't know!

Potential Is Everywhere Always

Understand this—everything you see in this universe, yourself included, is nothing but the expression of an infinite power. This power is forever flowing into and through you. Scientists will tell you that everything is energy. I choose to say that everything is Spirit.

Let Go And Let God

For centuries there has been a select group of people who are the real thinkers. These individuals have always known there is a power which permeates, penetrates and fills the interspaces of the cosmos, and that everything you see around you is an expression of that power. The power operates in a very precise manner, which is generally called law. In other words, everything comes from one source, and that source power always flows and works to and through the individual—that is you. Stated slightly differently, the image that you have formed can only come to you on the physical plane of life (your results) in one way, and that way is By Law and through Faith.

The Mormon religion has a scripture in its Doctrine and Covenants which demonstrates this point extremely well, and although I am not a Mormon myself, I have grown to love these lines:

"There is a law; irrevocably decreed in heaven before the foundations of this world upon which all blessings are predicated.

And when we obtain any blessing from God, it is by obedience to that law upon which it is predicated."

D & C 130:20-21

The more you study this scripture, the more you will appreciate just how perfect it is. The more you understand its truth, the easier it will be for you to improve the quality of your life.

Clarence Smithison's Story

A number of years ago, when I was working in Chicago, Illinois, I became close friends with a man by the name of Clarence Smithison. Since Clarence is not a celebrity, by any means, I am sure you have never heard his name before. In fact, he is such a modest, self-effacing person, that if he were to walk into a room crowded with people, you would probably not even notice him. Nevertheless, there is a certain indefinable spark in Clarence Smithison which makes him one of the most remarkable individuals I have ever had the pleasure to know. In an attempt to identify this elusive quality, I have come up with the following hypothesis: Clarence Smithison incorporates, within his very being, the principle upon which this entire chapter is based— namely, if a person will let go and let God (i.e. have faith that whatever must happen for him to achieve his goal, will indeed occur), all things become possible.

One day I confronted Clarence and asked him to share with me his view of faith and more specifically, his explanation of why he personally seemed to possess such a cornucopia of this important attribute. True to his nature, he explained to me he had not developed a complicated philosophy with respect to the subject. He said everything he believed about Faith could be summarized in a simple definition; and it was this definition which gave him the strength he needed to endure the trials and tribulations in his own life. "Faith," he said, "is the ability to see the invisible and believe in the incredible and that is what enables believers to receive what the masses think is impossible." I have fallen in love with this particular definition and have shared it with countless numbers of people, since Clarence first shared it with me.

Using a slightly different vocabulary, I would make the observation: "If you can show me a person who achieves great things, I can show you a person who has great faith in his God-given ability to achieve what he images." In fact, there is absolutely no question in my mind that faith has always been the miracle worker throughout history. It is the connecting link between God and You, and therefore, it is your most valuable nonphysical possession. In truth, it is the cornerstone to everything you will ever build or achieve during the course of your entire lifetime.

Comparatively few people today realize just how much faith in oneself (that part of oneself which is spiritual, perfect) has to do with achievement, because the great majority of people never seem to conceive of faith as being a genuine creative force. Yet the truth is that not only is Faith a bona fide power, but it is the greatest one we will ever encounter. In fact, I would go so far as to say that whatever you accomplish in your lifetime, will be in direct proportion to the:

1) intensity, and
2) persistence of your faith.

David And Goliath

Consider, for example, the biblical story of

David and Goliath, which surely must rank as one of the greatest testaments ever written on the subject of faith. As you will recall, Goliath, the giant of Gath, came into the Israelite camp boasting pompously and taunting the Israelites to select a man to do battle with him. The Israelites, naturally, were terrified and, not surprisingly, none of them leaped forward to accept the challenge.

Sometime later, however, when Goliath returned to reiterate his challenge, David, an Israelite youth, overheard the giant's obnoxious boasting and he stepped forward to pick up the gauntlet. Finally, after much pleading before his elders for the dubious honor of facing Goliath in battle, the youth was accorded the great "privilege" of going forth to do battle. The elders insisted, however, that David clothe himself in heavy protective armor. They also gave him a sword with which to smite his powerful adversary. But David said, "I am not used to these things, I cannot fight with these handicaps. These are not my weapons. I have other weapons with which to fight the giant." So he stripped himself of all his armor, and went into battle with no weapon other than a simple slingshot and a few pebbles which he had gathered from the nearby brook.

When the giant leader of the Philistines, protected as he was with armor from head to toe, armed with mighty weapons and preceded by his shield-bearer, saw the unarmed, unprotected Israelite youth approaching, he was infuriated. He said to David, "Come to me and I will give thy flesh unto the fowls of the air and to the beasts of the field." Young David, however, never one to be intimidated, answered the giant saying, "Thou comest to me with a sword and with a spear, and with a shield, but I come to thee in the name of the Lord of hosts, the God of the armies of Israel whom thou has defied. This day will the Lord deliver thee into mine hands." While the giant Goliath placed his faith in physical objects like armor, swords and shields, David placed his solely in an unseen God. The result—the young Israelite shepherd defeated his far mightier foe! With nothing, save a single stone from his sling, David struck Goliath, and the giant fell lifeless to the ground.

By accepting the principle "Let Go And Let God", and believing that whatever must happen for you to reach your goal, will happen—like David— you too will successfully conquer the "giant" in your life (i.e. you will witness the physical manifestation of your image, and in the proper time). You see, the trouble with those of us who fail to achieve what we desire, is not that we lack the ability to do so, but that we lack the faith implicit in the "Let Go And Let God" principle, which dictates whatever is necessary for us to reach our goal will indeed occur.

We do not believe we can simply tap into the great spiritual reservoir that lies within us, to make connection with divinity, all-supply, or whatever else you wish to call that power which sustains each one of us. However, if you fail to make this connection in your own mind, or if you lack the divine self-confidence born of faith in omnipotence, you will never be what you long to be, or have what you rightly deserve to have. All of your prayers will return to you unanswered; your best efforts will bear no fruit and your negative attitudes will thwart the realization of your goal.

A mind "saturated" with fear of failure or images of unwanted results, can no more accomplish, create, or produce anything of value, than a stone can violate the law of gravity by flying upwards in the air. You must realize the creator does not alter the law of gravity to accommodate a person who walks off the roof of a house. (Even though the person may do it unconsciously or in a drugged state.) Similarly, the creative principle of the law of achievement cannot be violated with impunity. Therefore, you will achieve what you desire, be what you long to be, only when you become obedient to that inexorable law of life.

To recapitulate—the first step in the creative process is to relax and see yourself already in possession of the good that you desire. (Build the image.) The second step is to—Let Go And Let God.

In working with Spirit, it helps to focus on the truth that Spirit is in all places at all times. Since this is so, it follows that you possess the godlike ability to tap into positive thoughts anytime you wish and anywhere you choose. Moreover, once you become aware of your kinship with the creative power, that you are in truth a child of spirit, you cannot possibly be anything other than positive, forceful, radiant and self-reliant in your dealings with the world (a conqueror of those forces which would attempt to drag you down or hold you back). Once this happens, all the forces in the universe will come together to help you reach your goal or the manifestation of your Image. Finally, gaining the understanding that you are made in the image of the creator of the universe—and are a living part of eternal spirit—will ultimately transform the results that you are achieving in your life, every day.

Another thing you should know about Spirit is that it is a power which is forever flowing into and through you (we also call this power "thought"). But as Spirit or thought flows into you, you choose the image you will then form with it. Experiment for yourself—sit back, relax and then become fully aware of this great creative capacity. You can actually form one image or picture, after another, on the screen of your mind (images of things which already exist physically, like your car, your home, your place of business, or images of things that do not yet exist—such as your short-term and long-term goals).

But the point I want to impress upon you now, is that although Spirit is the very essence of your being, it will never move into form or into an image, without your assistance. So those people who sit back and do nothing, saying, "God will look after me," are just fooling themselves. For since it is true that God helps only those who first help themselves, it follows that you must always do your part to start the creative process in motion. You must always build the image and know in your heart the image will materialize. You must come to look upon God as being a great unseen provider who inhabits every fibre of your being and you must also understand that the instant you form the image in your mind, God will go to work in God's Perfect Way and move you into an entirely new vibration (i.e. you will begin to feel differently). So always remember, the new feeling coming over you is really God at work and although you may sometimes express your elation by saying you feel enthusiastic, remember that the word Enthusiasm is just a derivation from the early Greek—"en theos"—meaning in God.

Your enthusiastic attitude will, in turn, cause your actions to change and you will start behaving differently. Moreover, not only will you begin to act differently yourself, but because of the new vibration you are in, you will begin to gravitate toward, and to attract to you, other like-minded people. Strange and wonderful things will begin to happen to you and with such regularity that you will be at a loss to explain or even to comprehend what is going on—so "don't even make the attempt." Just understand it is "God's Way," or "The Way of the Creative Force," and accept the good as it comes and expect more of the same in the future.

The skeptics will begin to say you are just lucky, and you should let it go at that. For as long as you continue to hold the image in your mind of the good you desire, you will always be rewarded. Just have faith that what should happen must happen, and in the right time, it will happen. Always remember that, the image which you keep affirming in your heart or your subconscious mind is being impressed upon Spirit, and Spirit has the ability to convert your present dreams into your future reality.

On the surface, it might appear, from time to time, that things are not going well and you may begin to worry you are moving in the wrong direction. But let me assure you, this will not be the case, as long as you keep the image of the good you desire firmly planted in your subconscious mind. For if you do this, you will continue to move in the only direction in which you can move, in order to get to where you want to go.

Don't forget, it is never sufficient to believe in yourself (that part of you which God created in His image) only when you feel particularly enthusiastic or when some particular good fortune has befallen you. It is never adequate to have FAITH sporadically; to get enthusiastic over your prospects and then to undermine all of your mental kingdom. It won't do to keep dropping down, again and again, like the frog trying to get out of a well, but is feeling weaker and more discouraged after each fall. Any person who starts that type of process in motion, is letting go of his Image of Prosperity and is using his creative powers to build images of poverty instead.

And as we have already said, God, being a just God, will always work to bring about your ultimate good. But always bear in mind it is your innermost thoughts and images you are requesting; not the words to which you might only be paying lip-service. Therefore, make it a habit to begin and end each day with A Declaration of Faith in yourself (created after God's image), and in His power (whatever you choose to call it). Guard this faith zealously, as you would your most precious possession and ensure that it never be imperilled by weak, downhearted and negative thoughts.

Doubts, fears, pessimism, and negative thinking poison the very source of life. They sap energy, enthusiasm, ambition, hope, faith and everything else which makes life purposeful, joyful and creative. You must consciously entertain only the mental allies of your ambition and those attributes which will help you realize the manifestation of your goal. For when you are firmly grounded in Faith, negative thoughts will have no power over you, because they will not be in harmonious vibration with your new image. You will be mentally strong through the conscious awareness of God's power within you.

When Times Get Tough

When things get tough you must get tougher and you can.

As Dr. Robert Schuller said, "Tough times never last, but tough people do." So if you find your faith slipping or you find yourself running low on this great motor power which accomplishes so many wonderful things, you can do something about it. The following exercise works for me—it has for years—and I know it will work for you too. You can build huge reservoirs of mental power by simply employing a daily autosuggestive technique, for the acquisition and the strengthening of this greatest and most necessary of all human attributes—Faith.

Note that when you are giving yourself this "mental treatment," you should always go off by yourself and speak out loud to yourself in a firm, decided tone of voice (verbalize what you are saying, just as earnestly as if you were speaking to someone else whom you wished to impress with the great importance of what you were asserting). When you speak to yourself, begin with your own name and continue as follows:

"YOUR NAME", You are a child of God and the being God made was never intended for the sort of weak, negative life you are leading. God made you for success not failure. God never made anyone to be a failure. You are perverting the great object of your existence by giving way to these miserable doubts of yourself, of your ability to be what you desire with all your heart to be. You should be ashamed to go out amongst your associates with a long, sad, dejected face, as though you were a misfit, as though you lacked creative power within, as though you did not have the ability to do what your Creator sent you here to do. You were made to express what you long to express. Why not do this? - why not stand and walk like a conqueror, like a David who slew Goliath, instead of giving way to discouragement and doubt and carrying on like a failure? The Image of Perfection, the Image of your Creator lies within you. You must bring it to the center of your conscious thought and express it to the world. Don't disgrace your Maker by violating that image, by being everything but the magnificent success God intended you to be."

There is a tremendous achievement force, an up-building and strengthening power in the asserting of confidence in the Creator and that you are created in His image.   This is not egotism, not the glorification of the parody of the man or woman which wrong-thinking or wrong-living has made. It is simply the assertion of your kinship with God.

Do Not Force It To Happen

There should be no force associated with the manifestation of your image, because "Force Negates." Trying to do it your way, by forcing things to happen, is not necessarily God's way. Therefore, learn to follow the quiet voice within that speaks in feelings rather then words; follow what you "hear" inside, rather than what others may be telling you to do. Be aware that the quiet voice within often tells you to do things which run counter to the way most people live their lives. But do not be unduly concerned by this. Many of the world's greatest leaders were considered heretics by their peers, simply because they chose to "march to the tune of a different drummer!" These individuals were following the quiet voice within them, rather than doing the things considered fashionable in their day.

Let your image sink deep into the treasury of your subconscious mind. Let yourself get totally and emotionally involved with your Image, because by doing this you are "Letting Go and Letting God."

Understand, moreover, that if you should falter—for any reason—and go your own way, the minute you recognize your error and reaffirm your image,

Spirit will pick up right where it left off when you chose to take over the controls. Then you will instantaneously be back in the right vibration and on the correct pathway, leading to success in life.

Follow the instructions on the next page, to the letter.

First Principle

*Relax and see yourself
already in possession
of the good that you desire.*

Second Principle

Let Go And Let God!

Chapter 5

EXPECT
AN
ABUNDANCE

EXPECT AN ABUNDANCE

"The mind is a powerful magnet and as such, it attracts whatever corresponds to its ruling state. Expectation dictates what that ruling state will be and therefore governs what corresponds to the mind and is attracted into your life. Expectation can be either a blessing or a curse but either way it is certainly one of the most powerful unseen forces in your life."

John Kanary
Public Speaker, Author, Entrepreneur

What are you doing to increase your income?

If your answer to this question is "nothing" or if you are just beginning to think seriously about what you could do, you have probably not yet grasped the ideas presented in the previous chapters. You should be aware that the chapters in this book resemble the individual pieces of a jigsaw puzzle. Each chapter is related, one to the other, in such a way that if we put them all together, we can see the entire picture. Since you are now well into the heart of the book, I would ask you to pay particularly close attention to the ideas which follow, so you can use them to successfully tie all the pieces together. You will soon discover that if the ideas in this chapter are applied with intelligence, Expectation can be the triggering mechanism which attracts into your life, every good you desire. However, if you do not exercise extreme caution, Expectation can also turn, just as rapidly, into a destructive, lethal enemy. Therefore, you must be cognizant of how you are

exercising this invisible, but powerful, force.
I believe you already understand you cannot have
wealth in your material world until you have first
visualized the wealth in your mind. But what does
this really mean? It means that before any of us can
even begin to overcome the poverty which surrounds
us in our external world, we must first conquer the
impoverishment that is buried deep within ourselves.

In the preceding pages, I explained how
prosperity—properly understood—is simply the
inward awareness of the opulence, wholeness and
completeness that abounds within the spiritual
realm. In other words, it is impossible to feel poor
when you are conscious of being enveloped in the
protective care of a loving God, universal spirit, or
whatever else you may wish to call the spiritual-
center of our universe. Let me repeat—there never
is, and there never has been any lack of supply other
than that which we have created for ourselves
because of our own limited awareness.

The Lightbulb Tale

The following story should help underscore this
great truth about your infinite source of supply.
Visualize, if you will, a poor couple who have spent
their entire lives living in the "backwaters" of
civilization. Then imagine them suddenly
transported to a small village where, to their
astonishment, they discover that their new home is
being lighted by "electricity." Since they have had
no previous experience with that force—in fact they
have never even seen an electric light before, they

are completely mesmerized by the little eight candlepower electric bulbs which light their home.

Several months pass by and eventually the couple start to regard the light-bulbs as an accepted facet of modern life. However, one day a smooth-talking salesman appears at their door, telling them their eight candlepower electric bulbs are no longer adequate for their needs. He tells them they should buy the new sixty candle-powered bulbs which have just "come on the market." Since the couple has now become slightly more adventuresome, they agree to let the salesman demonstrate his "newfangled" product. As soon as the new bulb is plugged in and the electricity turned on, the couple becomes transfixed once again; for not only does the new bulb emit a light, it actually illuminates the entire room. Never in their wildest fantasies had the couple ever imagined that the source of the new flood of illumination had been there all the time. Nor had they realized this enormously increased light could originate from the same current which fed their little eight candlepower bulb.

It's strange! We smile at the naivete demonstrated by this poor couple, but the truth is, most of us are even less aware of our own power, than this couple was of the power of electric current. For like the couple in the story, we never even dream that the infinite current which surrounds us could flood our lives with a light more magnificent than the most powerful light bulb ever devised. We never grasp the simple truth that all we need to do to improve our results is to plug a larger, more prosperous idea into the infinite current of life.

Instead, most of us strangle our supply with energy-impoverished thoughts of doubt and fear, which entirely cutoff the inflow of prosperity.

I want to exhort you, therefore, to resolve to change your habitual pattern of thinking now. That's right, change it now, and remember, the stream of plenty always flows towards the open, expectant mind. You must understand you already have in substance, if not in physical form, everything necessary to produce prosperity in your material world. The two determining factors for you to attain the results you want are:

1) desire, and
2) expectation.

Up to this point you might have been living the way the masses live their entire lives, simply because you are harboring the false assumption that desire is the only thing which you need to reach your goal. But you must understand, if your desire is not combined with the expectation that you will receive what you desire, you will find yourself continually frustrated and disappointed whenever you begin working toward any kind of material goal.

When you cast your mind back over the experiences of your own life, you will soon realize that whenever you did reach a desired goal, you not only desired that goal but you actually expected to attain it as well.

Let me repeat—desire without expectation is nothing more than wishful thinking and as we have already pointed out, since the vast majority of people wish positive but expect negative, they seldom attain what they are after.

In his magnificent book The Science of Getting Rich, the author, Wallace D. Wattles, gave us an excellent definition of "desire." He said: "Desire is the effort of the unexpressed possibility within seeking expression without through your action."

In other words, your ideal, dream or goal—this wealth you wish to see materialize—can only become a desire once it has been properly planted in the subconscious mind. However, once your desire has been firmly established, it is the expectant attitude which ensures that your goal or dream is not uprooted or replaced by any opposing or competing ideas.

In an effort to help you kindle this expectant attitude toward "real wealth," let us journey together through some of the preceding chapters in this book. As you will remember, we began by discussing "money." We attempted to understand the "true nature" of money and we arrived at the conclusion it is a "useful, obedient servant." However, like all servants, we learned it is useful to us only when it is being employed. Therefore, we concluded, money must always be kept working or otherwise circulating. For if it is not, as we have already mentioned, it will become as useless as old newspapers stashed away in an attic.

Next, we explored the idea relating to exactly "how much money you want." You become aware of the fact it is necessary to be very specific about how much money you need, to provide the things you want, to live in the style you choose. Once this figure had been decided upon, we then examined the importance of building the image of ourselves already in possession of this wealth, on the screen of our conscious mind. We also talked briefly about the manner in which images are formed and the role they play in our lives.

Then we examined the idea of "consciousness" and how it was imperative to develop the prosperity which we seek in our mind first, before we can ever attain it in our bankbooks. We learned how we had to bathe our subconscious minds in a concept of prosperity and how we had to see wealth as being already in our possession.

In the chapter "Let Go And Let God," we became aware we were co-creators. We became aware of how we had, in our conscious mind, the ability to choose any thoughts we wanted, to build any images which we chose to build. We then learned how we could turn that image over to our subconscious mind (the spiritual center of our being, and that part of us which takes any idea or image we give to it, then willingly accepts it and instantly begins to move it into physical form in our world). We discovered that when we truly understand this creative process of life and our role in it expectation becomes a natural mind-set, regardless of how things might appear in our outside world or what others might be saying to us. We were told this absolute and unshakeable faith or belief in the fact that our images are moved into form, is essential if we are to become successful in our lives. We also gained an awareness that all of this will happen once we begin to see ourselves as nonphysical entities encased in physical bodies. Once we realize our bodies are nothing other than the physical manifestation of our nonphysical selves, we will understand they are obedient servants of our mind, and they move and have their being according to the vibratory rate of our minds.

You must reach the stage in your mental development where you don't just believe that your image of material wealth will manifest in form, but you actually know it will. It is at that point you will begin to expect to receive the physical expression of your image of wealth. No one and no thing will be able to cause you to see in your mind anything but that. Always remember, the truth is not always in the appearance of things.

An elderly, wealthy gentleman being interviewed by a newspaper reporter was asked at what point he became successful. His answer was, "I was successful when I was sleeping on a park bench because I knew where I was and I knew where I was going." At this juncture in the book, you know where you are and you know where you are going. So expect to get there!

Your desire is the motorpower which will move you in the direction of your dream and expectation is the attractive force that will move your dream in your direction. So see yourself moving toward the wealth you visualize and see the wealth you visualize being attracted to you. Know that you will come in contact with the wealth that is moving to you, and at the right time. No one knows what period of time must elapse, so don't become impatient if it doesn't materialize "overnight." All we know for sure is a certain period of time must elapse and the period of time which your image must take to materialize is governed by the law of gender. The law of gender decrees there is a gestation or incubation period for the manifestation of all seeds, and, make no mistake about it, the image of wealth you chose to build on the screen of your conscious mind and then turned over to your subconscious mind is a seed; and it is growing into physical form, in the most fertile field of which you could ever conceive.

It is not necessary, at this point, for anyone else to see this new wealth. It is not even necessary for anyone else to believe you will receive it. The only thing necessary is that you see it and you believe it. You see, the premise that Napoleon Hill built his life's work on is absolutely true—anything the mind can conceive and believe, it will achieve. Expressed another way, "As a person thinketh in their heart, so are they." (The early Greeks referred to the subconscious mind as the heart.) Note that your subconscious mind can no more change or alter your image, than an ordinary mirror can reflect back to you an image different than the object you are holding in front of it. But remember, as you think so are you, does not mean as you tell people you think or as you would wish the world to believe you think; it means your innermost thoughts, which only you control, know the truth. That is what you expect, so that is what you attract and that is what you will ultimately receive!

Through studying the power of your subconscious mind, or studying in depth the power or modus operandi of Spirit, it will become easier and easier for you to come to expect the good you desire. For all things are possible in Spirit, because in its original state, Spirit is a sensitive, unseen, creative substance whose sole purpose is expansion and fuller expression; in other words, "growth." However, spirit or creative substance, can only reproduce, expand and express itself in a greater way in accordance with the limitation placed upon the instrument through which it expresses itself.

Since Spirit is flowing to and through you, you are the instrument. Therefore, the image or the ideas you hold in your mind dictate the limits which are placed on the spiritual power flowing to and through you. In this respect, you may be compared to the light bulb the elderly couple had in their home. You are an instrument through which spirit flows, just as a light bulb is an instrument through which electricity flows. When the old couple plugged in the eight candlepower bulbs, the electricity was limited in its expression by the power of the bulb. However, when the salesman plugged in the 60 candlepower bulb, the electricity was free to express itself to a greater degree, and yet even then it was limited by the form through which it flowed; namely, the new bulb. A 100 candlepower bulb would have permitted an even greater expression, and so on and so on. Therefore, if you held an image of poverty, that is what you will have seen expressed in your results or your material world. However, since you are now holding an image of prosperity, that is the image you will see expressed in your material world.

The nonphysical creative substance, which is Spirit, flows to and through the seed and expresses itself in its polar opposite, physical form. As we have discussed on previous pages, the modus operandi of Spirit is law and, of course the law of attraction is a cause, and growth or expansion is the effect. So keep visualizing yourself as a perfectly endowed spiritual instrument without limitations of any kind. For if you do, you will find it easy—in fact natural—to expect the good you desire. You will understand that doubt simply obstructs the unfoldment of your desire, so when you continually originate images of doubt, you know you will never see the materialization of the image you desire. Only the reproductive creative spirit of life knows what you think, until your thoughts become physical facts and materialize in your body or your affairs. Then everyone with whom you come in contact may know, because the intelligent energy rewards you openly by reproducing your thoughts in physical form.

As A Man Thinketh

"As you think, that is what you become," should be kept in the forefront of our minds constantly. For when you expect something wonderful to happen, that is watching and praying without ceasing. At those times when we are not feeling quite up to par physically or our mind is becoming clouded with doubt, we should realize it is time to pray with all the more conviction or work at developing a stronger feeling of expectation.

You must guard your mind constantly against doubt, because it is a crippling vibration. Whereas most of the preceding pages have been dedicated to the power of positive thoughts (namely, the building of the image of prosperity), doubt is the flip side of the coin (i.e. negative thinking). And, when you are entertaining doubts, what you are actually doing is creating images of the things you don't want. Moreover, justifying your doubt to yourself by originating reasons for it (i.e. rationalizing), will do you absolutely no good. You cannot strike a bargain with your subconscious mind, because the subconscious has no sense of fairness, no sense of humor, and it cannot even determine what is good or what is bad for you. Every image just IS, to the subconscious mind. Therefore, your negative, worrisome and doubtful images will be accepted just as quickly and as willingly as will your images of prosperity.

The instant you become aware you are entertaining thoughts which create doubt, become quiet, start relaxing and image yourself already in possession of the prosperity you desire. When you do this, you are altering the mental current which is flowing into your marvelous mind.

Expect, with all of your consciousness, to receive your good in your material world—"You think in secret and it comes to pass, environment is but your looking glass." James Allen wrote those words three-quarters of a century ago, but they are still true today and they will always remain true in the future.

So program your "personal computer" to expect good results and that is exactly what you will receive.

Pat And John's Story

As I was writing these lines, I received a telephone call from a beautiful couple—Pat and John—whom I would definitely number among my close friends. They called to tell me they were moving into their new home the following Tuesday, and I was elated to hear this delightful news. You see, less than two months earlier, I spent approximately five hours talking with them about the image-making concept and the awesome power of the "Expectant Attitude." During the course of the conversation, I asked John what he wanted more than anything else in the world, and, after a long period of silence, he looked me squarely in the eye and said, "I would like Pat, Toni (Pat's daughter) and me to be in a house of our own by Christmas and I would like my son to spend Christmas day with us." (Although John's son lives with his mother, he and John have a very warm relationship.) I then asked him why he didn't just go out and make his dream become a reality. He replied he couldn't, because he lacked the money to do so. I then had the audacity to remind John, that all things are possible for those who believe, and therefore, he definitely could make his dream come true; perhaps he just didn't know how to go about doing it. The three of us then spent about an hour discussing the kind of house they wanted, until we all had a very clear image of their dream home etched upon the screens of our minds. We talked about Expectation and I explained to them that many good things would begin to happen for them the instant that they began to "Expect" to be in the house for Christmas.

Sure enough, the first thing that happened to them once this new attitude permeated their consciousness, was that both their minds moved over to the "How To" side of the ledger. New ideas began to flow like water, and questions came forth in rapid succession. How much would a house like this cost? How much would they have to "put down?" Where would they find such a house? To get answers to their questions, they needed the expertise of a real estate agent; I suggested John call Natalie Kopman—a lady I know who is a real estate professional—and tell her of his dream. He should ask her what he would need in the way of finances to make his dream or image become a reality. Finally, I told him he would have to get busy focusing all of his conscious attention on earning the amount of money he would need to achieve his goal; and he would have to actually "Expect" to earn whatever the amount was—and in the allotted time. Surprisingly, it turned out that the amount of money they required was far less than the figure they had previously thought it would be.

Moreover, since John and Pat are both commissioned sales people, their road to achieving this financial goal was not riddled with as many obstacles as is the road for many other people. Nevertheless, without going into detail about the many hurdles they did have to overcome, suffice it to say, with Natalie's help, Pat and John succeeded. Next Tuesday they move into their new house, next Saturday is Christmas day. Just before I hung-up the receiver, I congratulated them on their new home and I asked John if his son would be spending Christmas day with them. Quietly, but with a voice brimming over with happiness, he answered, "Yes he is, and it sure makes a difference when you Expect what you do want, rather than Expecting what you don't want, doesn't it Bob?" I just smiled and said, "Yes John, it sure does."

Many people today live their entire lives on the basis of "seeing is believing." That is to say, the only images they get emotionally involved with are the ones they can discern with their physical senses. But the individuals of real "vision", down through the ages, have always known the overriding principle is, "What you see is what you get." Expressed somewhat differently, what this means is that the images in people's minds actually precede the concrete images which pervade our material world. Therefore, you should be aware of the fact that the fascinating physical world we see before us, with all of its conveniences for making our lives more comfortable, has been built largely by image-makers—men and women of vision who knew what they could do and "Expected" everything else to "fall into place," regardless of what their critics might say to the contrary.

For example, two young mechanics from Ohio introduced us to an entirely new kingdom by building and holding an image of an airplane in flight; but if they had not "Expected" to succeed, they would surely have quit the first time they met with defeat. Since they did not, we are now only hours away from anywhere in the world—in fact, we can even reach other planets within a very short span of time. Edison built and held an image which illuminated the entire world and, as a result, we no longer need to spend half of our days groping in darkness. You should realize that you too can change your world, just as John and Pat did, by building an image in your mind of exactly the way you would like to live. But always remember, you will only receive what you truly "Expect", not what you only wish for.

There are three certain steps for achieving prosperity in all areas of your life. Number one, build the image in your mind. Number two, turn it over to Spirit (Let Go And Let God). Number three, expect with your heart and soul that Spirit will reward you openly for your faith.

Expect An Abundance

Chapter 6

THE
LAW OF
VIBRATION
AND ATTRACTION

Thoughts Are Things

I hold it true that thoughts are things;
They're endowed with bodies
and breath and wings:
And that we send them forth to fill
The world with good results, or ill.
That which we call our secret thought
Speeds forth to earth's remotest spot,
Leaving its blessings or its woes
Like tracks behind it as it goes.

We build our future, thought by thought,
For good or ill, yet know it not.
Yet so the universe was wrought.
Thought is another name for fate;
Choose then thy destiny and wait,
For love brings love and hate brings hate.

Henry Van Dyke

THE LAW OF VIBRATION AND ATTRACTION

"Any idea that is held in the mind
that is either feared or revered will, begin at once
to clothe itself in the most convenient
and appropriate physical forms available."
Andrew Carnegie

Dr. Wernher von Braun

In an interview held with Dr. Wernher von Braun in February of 1976, Dr. von Braun was quoted as follows: "After years of probing the spectacular mysteries of the universe, I have been led to a firm belief in the existence of God. The grandeur of the cosmos serves only to confirm my belief in the certainty of a creator. I just cannot envision this whole universe coming into being without something like divine will. The natural laws of the universe are so precise that we have no difficulty building a spaceship to fly to the moon and can time the flight with the precision of a fraction of a second. These laws must have been set by somebody." Dr. von Braun went on to say, that "science" and "religion," properly understood, are not antagonistic pursuits. On the contrary, he affirmed, they are "sister disciplines." Through the scientific method, one learns more about "creation," whereas, by virtue of the study of religion, one gains a greater insight into the "creator." By employing the tools of science, man attempts to harness the forces of nature which surround him; through religion, on the other hand, he endeavors to control the "forces of nature," which are at work within him. After a brief pause, he added, "There would not be a single great accomplishment in the history of mankind without faith ... Any person who strives to accomplish something needs a degree of faith in himself and when he takes on a challenge that requires more and more moral strength than he can muster, he needs faith in God."

Years before anyone would accept the idea of a man travelling to the moon and back, Dr. von Braun was asked, "What would it take to make a rocket to reach the moon." He replied simply, "The will to do it." von Braun was, clearly, a brilliant man who possessed a great understanding of life and a tremendous awareness of the laws of the universe. In fact, he is considered, by many experts in the field, to be the "Father" of the space program. Like all great achievers, he had gained a profound insight into the "spiritual" laws of life, and one of those laws is the Law of Attraction. This is the law I would like to delve into now.

Indeed, an understanding of this particular law is actually the key to understanding this entire book. The reason this is so, is that "The Law of Attraction" is the underlying principle which governs the level of your personal prosperity. However, to help you achieve a really solid grasp of this concept, it will be necessary for us to focus briefly on another law; namely, the "Law of Vibration."

The Law of Vibration accounts for the difference between mind and matter; between the physical and the nonphysical worlds.

According to the Law of Vibration, we postulate that everything vibrates or moves; nothing sits idle. Everything is in a constant state of motion, and therefore, there is no such thing as "inertia", or a state of rest. From the most ethereal, to the most gross form of matter, everything is in a constant state of vibration.

Moving from the lowest to the highest degree of vibration, we discover there are literally millions upon millions of intervening levels or degrees; from the electron to the universe, everything is in vibratory motion. (Energy is manifested in all the varying degrees of vibration.)

"Rates of vibration" are called "frequencies," and the higher the frequency, the more potent the force. Since thought is one of the highest forms of vibration, it is very potent in nature and therefore, it must be understood by all of us.

Now, the Law of Vibration may be explained in many different ways, depending upon the purpose for which it is being explained. In this chapter, however, it is our intention to confine our inquiry to thoughts alone, so we may thereby improve our understanding of the Law of Attraction.

Vibration

To vibrate means:
"to move backwards and forwards, to oscillate, to shake, to quiver, to swing, to waver, to cause to quiver."

To obtain a more graphic conceptualization of the idea of Vibration, just stretch out one of your arms straight in front of you. Then hold it perfectly still. While you are holding it still and are unable to perceive any motion in that arm at all, know that the electrons which compose the arm, are moving, shaking, quivering, or vibrating, at the rate of 186,300 miles per second.

The arm appears still to you, but in reality it is in a constant state of motion. Of course, although such motion is imperceptible to the naked eye, under a high-powered microscope it would become very apparent, indeed.

Now, begin to shake your arm. You, yourself, are now causing the arm to vibrate. It was already vibrating of its own accord, in obedience to the Law of Vibration (which teaches that everything is in constant motion). But you have stepped up, or increased, the rate of that vibration. You have pushed down on the vibratory accelerator pedal, as it were.

Positive And Negative Personalities

"The mind in itself and in its own place
can make a hell out of heaven
or a heaven out of hell."
John Milton

People, as a rule, can be classified as positive personalities (optimists) or negative personalities (pessimists).

Those individuals who are positive in their thoughts always tend to look upon the brighter side of life. With their faces turned toward the sunshine, they attempt to see the good, even in the bad. Such individuals habitually think thoughts of a positive nature and they are a blessing to the world. They are in a "Positive Vibration," and therefore attract other positive personalities to them.

Negative personalities, on the other hand, habitually look upon the dark, gloomy, and depressing side of life. Even the good holds some bad for them. They dwell on the bad and the negative. They think about it, anticipate it, expect it, and invariably they receive what they have been seeking. Due to the negative vibration which they keep themselves in, they of course attract other miserable personalities to them. As you are already aware, "misery loves company."

Their state of mind can be compared to the person who, upon being asked how he felt, said,

"I feel alright today,
but I might feel bad tomorrow."

Negative personalities are depressing to everyone around them. Their faces take on the expression, in physical form, of the negative thoughts which they are holding in their minds. Each day, one can observe such individuals passing on the street. No cheer, no joy radiates from them— just gloom, frowns and hostility. Having created their own hell for themselves, they seem to enjoy wallowing in it.

The law of Polarity and Relativity states that for every positive there is an equal and opposite negative. Therefore, both of these personality types are necessary, so you can develop the awareness to distinguish one from the other, and in that manner, choose the one which will advance you in life.

You do have Free Will. You can choose which of these two personality types you wish to adopt. Therefore, if a person is constantly negative, but tires of that state, the person may, through awareness and proper effort, change himself into a positive personality type of individual.

Understand this—The Law of Vibration will give people the awareness they require, to make the personality changes they desire.

The Brain — The Body

The human body, believe it or not, is one of the most efficient electrical instruments in this entire universe. The human brain, similarly, is probably the most efficient electrical instrument ever created. Both are truly marvels.

The brain is the part of the body where all manner of frequencies are transformed from one frequency level into another. In the brain, for example, sensations are transformed into muscular action. Sound, heat, light and thought are also, each in their turn, transformed into other frequencies, each affecting the body.

Within the brain there are centers which control

and regulate the functioning of all organs and parts of the body. By means of the proper stimulation of these centers, the functioning of the organs may thereby be controlled. In our seminars, we refer to this phenomenon as the vibratory control of the body.

In the final analysis, the brain is simply a vibratory instrument. To begin to understand its functioning you must undertake the study of the Law of Vibration.

Since the early 1940's, we have had at our disposal the EEG (electroencephalograph), which reads the electrical activity of the brain, and the ECG (electrocardiograph), which traces the electrical changes which occur during heart contractions.

Therefore, vibrations are certainly not something which are new to us. Indeed, all of us have an awareness of them. However, the problem which we encounter is that the vast majority of people are not aware of the connection between their vibrations and their results in life.

It is, unfortunately, a very common sight to see people in bad or confused vibrations, busily attempting—through force—to achieve good results. However, due to the negative vibration which they are in, they are continually being bombarded by all manner of negative people and situations, which by law, are being attracted to them. Consequently, at some point, their battle must become overwhelming for them.

These people may be likened to a person who is jumping off the top of a building, and trying to go up, at one and the same time. The result, in either case, would be equally predictable and equally disastrous.

Everything Is Energy, Everything Vibrates

For you to gain a better awareness of how you are to take control over your results (i.e. to better understand how and why the thoughts and things come into your life as they do), you must go back to the basic premise with which we started: namely, everything vibrates and nothing stands still. There is, in truth, no such thing as inertia. Scientists today support this thesis and every new scientific discovery tends to lend even more credibility to it.

However, by virtue of your Free Will and the many other mental factors in your marvelous mind, you have the Co-Creative ability to cause vibratory changes to take place at your bidding in your life. The cause for our lack of ability to exercise this tremendous power for good is nothing other than our own ignorance about the Law of Vibration.

Let There Be Light—Your Connecting Link

Slowly but surely, let us see with our inner eye of understanding, how you may "connect" with the good that you desire, to improve the quality of your own life.

Two objects whose electromagnetic fields are the same are operating on the same frequency.

Therefore, we can say they are in resonance, in harmony, or in rapport. When two objects are in resonance or vibrating at the same speed, the vibratory rate may be transmitted from one to the other through the medium of the electron. ("Resonance" as a field of study, is concerned with the electromagnetic fields surrounding objects.)

For example, we find a globe in a chandelier will vibrate when in resonance with a certain key on a piano; yet it will not vibrate to any other note on the piano keyboard.

The two objects under discussion are composed of entirely different material and they have completely different shapes. Still, they are in resonance with one another, due to the fact their ultimate magnetic fields are the same. They are within the same sphere of relative motion, and this holds true, irrespective of their size, shape, or the elements of which they are composed.

All electromagnetic waves, or quantums, have their own particular rate or frequency, which corresponds to the number of changes in direction they make per second. The electromagnetic wave spectrum is simply a "Scale of Vibration," and it is subdivided into specific regions.

Nevertheless, one must always remember these regions are not actual divisions, but merely arbitrary spaces covering frequencies that manifest in our senses in different ways. Each region actually "blends" into the one above and the one below, and in truth, there are no definite lines of demarcation.

Everything Is An Expression Of The Same Thing

Everything in this entire universe is connected to everything else in this entire universe, through the Law of Vibration. Just as the colors in a rainbow are connected in such a way that you are not able to tell where one color stops and the other begins, so too are you unable to distinguish where one "thing" starts and another one stops. Everything in this universe is connected to everything else in this universe, just as the water that boils is connected to the steam into which it transmutes, and the steam is connected to the ether or air into which it changes.

You too are connected to everything in the universe. Whether you can see it with the naked eye or not is unimportant. The only physical difference which exists between one thing and another, relates to the density or the amplitude of their vibration.

Therefore, as soon as you choose certain thoughts, your brain cells are affected. These cells vibrate and send off electromagnetic waves. When you concentrate on those thoughts, you increase the amplitude of vibration of those cells, and the electric waves, in turn, become much more potent.

Know that it is you who is originating those electric waves and know that you are also determining the density of them by your own free will. You must also know, since you are originating these electric waves, your whole being is being put in that particular vibration.

We have already covered the point that two objects may be of entirely different material and shape, and yet still be in Resonance. This is due to the fact their ultimate magnetic fields are the same, because they are within the same sphere of relative motion. (Keep in mind that resonance is the factor governing the transmutation of vibrations.)

When you hold the image of your goal on the screen of your mind, in the present tense, you are vibrating in harmony (in resonance) with every particle of energy necessary for the manifestation of your image on the physical plane. By holding that image, those particles of energy are moving toward you (attraction) and you are moving toward them— because that is the law.

All things are merely manifestations of energy or Spirit.

When the world comes to understand this great truth, we will be aware that all people are the same; they only appear to be different. The true dividing lines for mankind are not borders, color or language, but simply ignorance and its polar opposite, understanding.

KNOW THE TRUTH
AND THE TRUTH WILL SET YOU FREE.

Helping Others Feel Better

You automatically like people who cause you to

feel good. It would necessarily follow, therefore, that others will like you when you cause them to feel good, or when you move them into a more positive vibration.

Example

Vibratory control of the body, mind and soul of a person gives you a means for the restoration of positive vibrations, through the medium of resonant electric waves of the brain cells, from you to another person.

As already stated, the human body, including the brain, is a high-powered electrical instrument. Therefore, you are a veritable "broadcasting station," relative to other people. When the "tune in" between you and them has been completed, or when the composite personality has been established between you and the other person, the other person receives and becomes conscious of the vibrating thought which is being broadcast by you.

Under the Law Of The Perpetual Transmission And Transmutation Of Energy, the other person, being a low potential of energy, takes on this added energy which is being sent out by you. And, like a weak battery, the other person becomes recharged, more energetic, and more positive as a result of his contact with you.

The process of transmitting energy between you and the other person is exactly the same as the process which takes place between the broadcasting station and the radio. That is to say, laws which are identical in nature, govern both phenomena.

Vibrations And Attitude

Every physical thing throws off a vibration. Everything which you see, hear, smell, taste, or touch, throws off a vibration because these things, like everything else, are in a constant state of motion. Whenever you get near enough to them to enter into their "sphere of vibration," you will be affected by that vibration, whether you realize it or not. Have you ever noticed, for example, how peaceful you feel (vibrate) while walking alone in the woods?

The Law operates exactly in the same way in the mental realm. For when a person thinks a thought, it means the person has consciously or unconsciously started a group of brain cells vibrating abnormally. Once these brain cells, being things, begin to vibrate abnormally, they throw off a wave of electronic energy which moves out seeking a place to land.

If you are in the sphere (space) of their vibrations and you happen to have similar cells which are in rapport (in harmony or agreement) with the ones vibrating in the other person's brain, then you receive these vibrations and are affected mentally by them, either negatively or positively. (It is clear that everyone in sales or management will thoroughly understand this information.)

Let us suppose that another person is vibrating to "Anger Concepts." If you are the type of person who becomes easily angered and you happen to enter the vibratory field of those anger vibrations, then those vibrations will strike the "anger cells" in your own brain. A condition of resonance being present, those vibrations will start your brain cells vibrating and your entire being will move into that vibration. You will become irritated or angry (even though you may, or may not know, the cause of your own anger). If you do not understand what has happened, you will be at a loss to change the conditions which caused the effect in the first place.

The same principle applies to all mental vibrations. As soon as a person starts to think, he starts brain cells vibrating. Energy is released, therefore, in the form of electrons which travel out according to the intensity of the thought involved. Whoever stops that energy, is affected by it. But bear in mind, the only thing which stops a thought, is that which resonates with that thought. This means, if you should run into an electromagnetic vibratory field of negative thoughts, you will, if you are that type of person, become negative yourself. Conversely, if you run into a positive vibratory field, you will experience the opposite of the negative; namely, the positive.

Since the air we breathe is literally "filled" with both types of vibrations, they are constantly bouncing into your brain. As a result, you could become like a "ship without a rudder," tossed about at the mercy of whatever is vibrating or "in the air." However, once you understand the Law of Vibration, you are in a position to insulate yourself against the negative vibrations. You can then be in control of yourself, in the true sense of the word, and you will begin to attract to you the things and circumstances that you choose.

Become A Mental Magnet

Attract What You Need
For The Physical Manifestation Of Your Image

If it is true that energy, or Spirit, is neither created nor destroyed and everything in its original state is either energy or Spirit, it necessarily follows that everything you will ever want is already here. It is simply a matter of choosing the thoughts which will put you into harmonious vibration with the good that you desire.

Everything you are seeking is seeking you in return. Therefore, everything you want is already yours. So you don't have to get anything; it is simply a matter of becoming more aware of what you already possess.

The moment you bring your life into harmony with the Law, into harmony with the current of Divine Order, you will find that the "negative" will have "taken wings." For its cause will have been removed and you will no longer attract what you don't want.

The secret to receiving, on the physical plane, the results you desire is always locked into the Law of Attraction. This entire book has been designed to help you understand how to get into harmonious vibration with the good you desire, and then how to stay in that positive vibration, so you will begin to attract whatever you need for your image of prosperity to move into form.

The Acorn Analogy

In Raymond Holliwell's magnificent book, Working with The Law, Holliwell points out in the chapter entitled "The Law of Success," the following: "All of the processes of nature are successful. Nature knows no failures. She never plans anything but success. She aims at results in every form and manner. To succeed in the best and fullest sense of the term we must, with nature as our model, copy her methods. In her principles and laws we shall discover all the secrets of success."

Keep in mind that everything in this universe you can see with the naked eye and everything you cannot see, is an expression of Spirit. Also bear in mind that Spirit operates by exact laws. You are subject to those laws, in just the same manner nature is. Therefore, Holliwell is right—we definitely should copy nature's methods.

For years I have held up an acorn in the seminar and used it as a device for helping people to gain a better understanding of how the law of attraction actually works in their lives. So please visualize, if you will, an acorn. Then think—really think—about what it is you are looking at.

Although the acorn may appear to be a solid object, by now you should clearly understand that the acorn, like everything else which appears to be solid, is in truth, "a mass of molecules at a very high speed of vibration." Within the acorn, there is a nucleus or a patterned plan that dictates the vibratory rate at which these molecules will move. Moreover, the same principle holds true for all seeds. In other words, every seed has a nucleus or a patterned plan within it, which dictates the vibration it will be in and which thereby governs the end-product into which it will expand or grow.

I believe you are all aware of this fact: everything in the universe is governed by a basic law—"Either create or disintegrate." Therefore, it follows that, if something is not in the process of growing, it must, by the law of its being, be dying. For example, so long as the acorn is kept out of the earth, it is slowly but surely disintegrating. However, as soon as you plant the acorn in the earth, the patterned plan or the vibratory rate of the acorn sets up an attractive force and the acorn begins to attract everything that vibrates in harmony with it. If you were able to observe with the naked eye exactly what is taking place, you would see a "parade" of particles of energy—a never-ending stream of them—marching in a very orderly manner toward the acorn. As they came in contact with the molecules making up the acorn, they would join, marry, become one, and of course, the acorn would expand, become larger, grow.

Now consider this—if you were to put two drops of water and two drops of oil on an arborite table and then you were to move them together, the two drops of water would resonate and become one larger drop of water, as they came in contact with each other. On the other hand, if you were to move the water toward the oil, they would actually repel each other because they are not in harmonious vibration. Likewise, with the acorn, the only things which join with the acorn are those particles of energy which are vibrating in harmony with it. All the other particles of energy, which make up the earth, are repelled.

As the acorn expands from the never-ending stream of molecules which are attracted to it, little shoots begin to come out of the bottom and out of the top of it. These shoots, in turn, begin to develop into roots. As they grow or expand and burst through the earth into the earth's atmosphere, this attractive force continues, and particles of energy from the atmosphere are attracted to it (just as the particles of energy in the earth were attracted to it). As the acorn continues to expand, at some point it ceases to be an acorn and it begins to become an oak tree. The roots, the trunk, the bark, the branches, the twigs, and the leaves, are all in the universe and they are attracted to the acorn, because of the nucleus or the patterned plan which rests within the seed.

Now, unlike the human creature, the acorn does not have the ability to change its vibratory rate. It can therefore only grow into what it has been programmed to grow into; namely, an oak tree. You are much like the acorn in many respects. For example, you are also a "seed," relative to the whole scheme of things. However, the difference between you and the acorn is that since you are a co-creator, you can choose your own programming. Therefore, the image you choose to hold, on the screen of your conscious mind, and plant deeply in the treasury of your subconscious mind is the patterned plan or the nucleus which determines what you will eventually grow into. It dictates the vibration you will be in and also controls what you will attract to you and what you will repel.

This is an orderly universe; nothing happens by accident. The images which you plant in your marvelous mind instantly set up an attractive force, which governs your results in life. You must remember though, if your image is continually fluctuating, you will continually be growing into something different and that sets in motion a most chaotic process. Unfortunately, those individuals who are unaware of these very exact laws are planting images of plenty in their minds one minute and then images of poverty the next. They are continually "switching" vibrations, so they are attracting good things one minute and then bad things the next. The sad truth is, the vast majority of people spend their entire lives oscillating between these two extreme positions, with the resulting effect that their lives become disordered and chaotic to the "nth" degree.

Although it is true that everything you will ever want is already here, it is up to you to get into harmony with it. Clearly, you will never get into harmony with prosperity, if you insist upon holding images of lack and limitation in the storehouse of your marvelous mind. Since you are always magnetized toward something, it follows it can never be anyone else's fault, when something comes into your life you supposedly do not want. Understand you have ordered it and it is being delivered to you, right on schedule!

BOB PROCTOR'S
MENTOR STUDY
PROGRAM

Would you like to be in Bob Proctor's personal mentoring program? You could study with him every week. He will compound both your income and effectiveness.

CALL
800-759-4136

Chapter 7

THE
RISK-TAKERS

THE RISK-TAKERS

The days of defending your present "possessions" and "positions" are gone forever. Therefore, from this day forward, you will never have to concern yourself with such problematic issues as "maintaining your present job", or "keeping up your current standard of living." Instead, you will put the things which "can go wrong" on the defensive, and you will put the things which "must go right", in ready formation for the attack. As of today, you are a dynamic, vigorous risk-taker, whose eyes are always turned toward your strengths and assets, rather than toward your weaknesses and liabilities. Henceforth, you will wake up in the morning, thinking only of "ways to do the things you want to do", rather than waking up thinking of "all the reasons why you cannot do those things."

As of today, you will think repeatedly of the many achievements which you are going to accomplish in the future, that are vastly superior to anything you have ever done in the past. Clearly, these are the results that can only be obtained if you are first willing to take some kind of a risk. Believe me, once you undertake this process, it won't be long before you start winning—and in a big way. You should understand, however, that as you become increasingly involved in the risk-taking process, you will find yourself forced to draw upon resources which you previously didn't even realize you possessed. At first, this may prove very frightening to you. Nevertheless, you must always remember you will never hear of, read about, or see anyone who achieves anything of greatness in his or her own life, without first taking some kind of a risk.

As a case in point, just consider the monumental risks which all of our great religious leaders have undertaken during the course of their heroic lives. Then stop and reflect upon the enormous risks which all of our great business leaders have also undertaken, during the span of their illustrious careers. Finally, as you seriously meditate upon these stupendous accomplishments, you will become increasingly aware of the fact that you too must become a risk-taker for you to develop the greatness you were born with. Moreover, you should understand, that in truth, no genuine satisfaction in life can ever be attained by you or anyone else, who simply refuses to take risks. For the life of anyone who chooses to live with extreme caution will never amount to anything more than a succession of dull, soporific days, continuing on, without interruption.

The Diving Board Analogy

To help you grasp the full implication of what I am saying, consider the following analogy. Just cast your mind back to the time when you were a child and attempt to recall the degree to which you admired "the neighborhood kid" who went right up the ladder, and dived off the high diving board without any hesitation whatsoever. Then see if you can recall the feelings which you harbored in yourself, as you watched him take that first "risky" leap into the water below. If you are like most of us, you probably lost just a little bit of your own self-respect at that time, until finally, out of sheer embarrassment, you too mustered up enough courage to jump. Finally, see if you can recollect how good you felt once you actually made the plunge and proved to the world that you could do it too.

Now that you have taken your mind on this mental journey through your past, bring it forward to the present time. Let it become fully aware of the legions of men and women today who—like the young child looking longingly at the high diving board—would dearly love to quit their jobs, set out on an independent path and do their own thing. However, due to their overwhelming fear of failure, these unfortunate people never quite work up enough courage to step out and actually take the plunge. As a result, such individuals miss out on many of the opportunities that life affords us all, and what is even sadder, they never get a chance to plumb "the depths" of their own innate resources. Since they are afraid they might not make it, afraid they might lose, afraid they might fail, they simply choose to maintain the status quo and do nothing. The irony is, however, that even if a person should assiduously attempt to avoid all risks, he or she will still inevitably end up failing from time to time! But the point is, so what? What difference does it really make? After all, "failing" does not make us a "failure", and the only time we do become a failure is when we decide to stop trying any more. Therefore, even if we should falter along the way, we never really fail because we always retain the capacity to try once more.

Flip Wilson's Story

Flip Wilson, the famous comedian, is best known for his ability to make people laugh. But here is what he said in a somewhat more serious vein, about his own experience with the risk-taking process. "I fell down and got up, I fell down and got up. For sixteen years I did practically nothing else but fall down and get up."

Even so, do you think Flip Wilson ever thought of himself as a failure? You bet your life he didn't. For if he had, he would never have found the courage to try "just one more time," and you and I would probably have never even heard his name!

You should understand, at this juncture, that as soon as you seriously set a big goal for yourself, you are going to become involved in a process of risk-taking which will add a dimension of excitement, indeed a whole new flavor to the course of your life. But at the same time you should be aware that as you start engaging in more risk-taking behavior, the majority of people will be trying to avoid it "at all costs." In other words, instead of taking meaningful risks, most people will continue to ensure themselves in a series of empty compromises. These compromises, in turn, will ultimately have the effect of reducing their existence to the level of a meaningless charade. To understand how this phenomenon operates, just consider the people whom you know who have compromised when buying their new home. "Why did they compromise?" you ask—because they were afraid that they wouldn't be able to make the mortgage payments on that "dream home" they truly wanted to live in.

Then turn your mind to the veritable armies of individuals, who remain in positions at work which they find dull and unrewarding. Why do they stay?— simply because they fear they would not be able to "cope with" the position which they would truly love to "tackle." The irony is, of course, if these people would simply put themselves "out on a limb"—by going after that better job or, that dream home, or whatever else it is they truly desire—they would then demand a commensurately better performance from themselves. As a result, they would soon discover that the risk they had taken was actually paying big dividends in all aspects of their life.

The Young Millionaires

Several years ago, I read an excellent book on the subject of risk-taking. It was entitled The Young Millionaires, and it contained the true-life stories of eighteen individuals, each of whom had earned in excess of one million dollars. In fact, some of these people had actually earned many millions of dollars, over and above the one million dollar mark, during the course of their highly successful careers. Throughout the book, the author made many interesting observations about the "law of financial success," but the most important one was the one which he kept coming back to: namely, although these individuals came from a variety of different backgrounds and although each had earned their money in a different way, they all shared one thing in common.

"What was that one thing?" you ask. Simply put, it was this—even though everything they owned was riding on the outcome of virtually every major business decision which they made, none of them considered themselves to be taking "risks." The reason they didn't, he went on to explain, was because they were living their lives "as though it were impossible to fail!" (Note, however, that in the eyes of most people, there would be no question that these individuals were taking tremendous risks—and on an almost daily basis).

Fighter-Pilot Study

In a similar vein, research done many years ago which investigated the lives of fighter pilots in World War II, determined conclusively that, contrary to what you might think, many of the pilots who "played it safe" during the war, were among the first to be killed in combat. By way of contrast, the study also found that, practically without exception, not only were the surviving aces individuals who refused to "play it safe," but they were the greatest risk-takers throughout the war. Indeed, as one has the opportunity to observe the performance of individuals from all walks of life, it soon becomes evident that whoever "plays it safe" in life, dies, and dies relatively young. For although many of these individuals remain "clinically" alive for numerous years, when their hearts finally cease beating it is a mere formality, because the truth is, they have never really lived!

By now you have probably said to yourself, "All of this sounds eminently reasonable, but why should it be?," or "Why are so many of us destined to go through our entire lives in this condition of self-imposed misery, simply because we are unable, or unwilling, to take meaningful risks?" Well, it seems to me if we will only cast our minds back to the formative years of our own lives, we will soon recognize where this reluctance to engage in risk-taking behavior has its source. Once we have arrived at that point, I believe we will have come a long way in our attempt to combat, and ultimately neutralize, this insidious problem. I exhort you to pay very strict attention to the information which will now be set-out before you.

When you were a young child—in fact, even as far back as the time when you were an infant—your parents desperately wanted to see you succeed. As a consequence of this wish, they were terrified by the prospect you might somehow fall short of their expectations of you. This was perfectly natural, in light of the fact they loved you very dearly. Unfortunately, however, it motivated them to attempt to shelter you from every potential harm which might come up in your life. For example, when you first started to walk, they were right by your side and as soon as you even looked like you were going to stumble, they quickly grabbed onto you, so you would not fall and hurt yourself.

Similarly, when you engaged in your first fist fight with "the little terror next door," your parents were there to soothe the bruised feelings. They probably tried to console you by saying "You were right dear, and the other wrong - the other child was a bully." Next, they probably said something like,

"In the future, dear, be very careful and try to stay away from kids like that." Moreover, if your upbringing was typical of that of most of us, your first bicycle probably brought with it repeated warnings such as: "be careful," "don't fall," "watch out," and so on. In this manner, you were slowly but surely "programmed" to make every move in your life with a brilliant caution light burning brightly on the screen of your impressionable young mind.

You must gain the awareness, therefore, that regardless of what anyone may have told you to the contrary, none of us was ever "born" with a fear of taking risks. As I have clearly indicated above, the fear of taking risks is something which we learned, only after we entered this wonderful world of ours. In fact, contrary to what many people have mistakenly been led to believe, the human being— if left to his or her own devices—is a born risk-taker who is "naturally" programmed to follow the path which will eventually lead to greatness in his or her own life.

But, be that as it may, before you embark on this exciting path of risk-taking, you should remember to never lose sight of the fact that becoming a risk-taker does not mean becoming an irresponsible individual. If you really think it through, you will realize these two concepts are mutually exclusive. For becoming a risk-taker means to act courageously, and to act courageously is considerably different from acting foolishly (which is how a person acts when he or she behaves in an irresponsible manner). You might encounter a few situations where the line separating these two concepts becomes extremely narrow. Nevertheless, it is absolutely essential you never cross over that line, inadvertently, or otherwise!

Another thing which you must be aware of, is that risk-taking is always a relative term. In other words, behavior which represents a risk to one person may not necessarily represent a risk to another person. Moreover, if the same behavior were carried out by a third party, one might even be tempted to deem it irresponsible conduct. It is clear, therefore, that one must be able to distinguish among these different concepts with a significant degree of accuracy. In order to achieve this, it becomes necessary to go back to one of the basic principles involved in the process of self-development.

You must be able to see yourself, with your inner eye, already in possession of the good you desire.

Risk-Taking vs. Irresponsibility

People who are irresponsible very rarely accomplish anything of importance and quite often they invite real harm to themselves. They might occasionally become involved in some activities which are successful, but these results occur so infrequently, and they are so overshadowed by negative results that they are hardly even worth mentioning.

Consider, for example, the individual who dives off a high cliff and into a shallow body of water, simply because he has been "dared" to do so by a group of his peers. Although the person in question is afraid to dive, for some strange reason he is even more afraid of what the others might say to him, or even think about him, if he chose not to dive. Clearly, the person's fear of diving is perfectly reasonable, in view of the fact he has had absolutely no training as a diver. Furthermore, as a result of his lack of training, when he does contemplate what might happen if he did dive, he visualizes himself being very seriously injured. Obviously, for an individual such as this to go ahead and dive, would be extremely foolish—to say the least—and the person's actions would have to be considered irresponsible by anyone's standards.

On the other hand, however, if this same person trained to become a professional diver and if he were skilled at taking all of the various factors into consideration (i.e. if he were able to visualize himself successfully going through all of the necessary motions such as swimming to shore, stepping back on land unharmed, etc.), then it would be a totally different situation. For although the person would still be taking a definite risk, no one could accuse him of acting in an irresponsible manner.

Consider for a moment, the "stunt people" who work in the movie industry. These individuals are constantly performing dangerous acts. In fact, that is precisely what they get paid for. But do not be deceived! For the men and women who perform these stunts are not amateurs by any means. They are all competent professionals, highly skilled in the performance of their dangerous trade. They always check and then double check every calculation, before they make even the simplest move. As a result of these precautions, they are very rarely ever injured. No, there cannot be any question about it—stunt people are "Risk-Takers" to be sure, but they are very rarely irresponsible individuals!

Investments

Now, turn your attention to the person who invests his or her hard-earned savings in a venture about which he or she knows practically nothing. Perhaps someone, possibly a relative whom the person may have held in high esteem, suggested this investment was a great idea and the investors stood to earn an extraordinarily high rate of return on it. Assume, moreover, that despite the person's very grave misgivings about going into the venture at all, he is also being strongly motivated by greed, to seek the highest possible rate of return which can be earned on the money invested. Finally, suppose that the tremendous fear of loss notwithstanding, the person decides to go ahead and makes the investment anyway. What happens next?

After the investment has been made, most of the person's waking hours will probably be spent:

1) worrying about the investment, and
2) visualizing himself reduced to a state of abject poverty.

It is abundantly clear, therefore, that this sort of behavior must be deemed the polar opposite of financial responsibility and the person involved must be considered imprudent and irresponsible, rather than a "bona fide" risk-taker. The usual outcome in a situation such as this is predictable, if not pleasing. The individual in question loses the money, not to mention the former friendship of the individual who originally suggested the investment. (The reason is that foolish, irresponsible people seldom blame themselves for making such errors.)

On the other hand however, if that person listened carefully to the suggestion of his friend or relative and then studied the situation for himself, he could have formed an opinion which was based on sound knowledge rather than hearsay, and which was motivated by genuine interest rather than simple greed. At that point, the individual could have gone ahead and invested a sum of money which would not have placed his total financial situation in jeopardy. Then, as he gathered more information based on actual experience, he could have gradually increased his investment if such action appeared to be in his best interest.

Clearly, if our hypothetical individual followed this second course of action, he would still certainly be taking a risk. However, one could not justifiably say he was behaving in the manner of a fool or an irresponsible person. Moreover, even in the eventuality that this person made a bad "judgement call," and lost his money, that would have been all he had lost. For he would still have his friendship and he would still have his own self-respect, because he would realize he had been guilty of nothing more than an error in judgement. An added benefit of this second approach is that the individual would not automatically reject future investment possibilities, should they arise.

I am sure you are getting my message "loud and clear": risk-takers are knowledgeable people who study situations carefully, have confidence in their own abilities and have a very healthy self-image. Put more succinctly, we can say risk-takers, unlike irresponsible people, are "nobody's fool."

Business Failures

Consider this—if one were to examine the statistics regarding the number of business failures each year, without closely studying each situation separately, one could very easily conclude that going into business for oneself is an "irresponsible act." However, that is just not the case! The truth of the matter is, many of the people who have gone into bankruptcy, should never have gone into business for themselves in the first place, either because they weren't properly prepared for such an undertaking or because they simply didn't know what they were doing. They lacked the skill, the knowledge, or the proper support to get their business "off the ground." Bear in mind that although it takes most new companies at least three years before they are properly established, some of these individuals didn't allow for three months, or even three weeks, to give their business a chance.

It is also significant to note, that prior to setting out on their own, many of these people were those employees who thought their boss was incompetent, or the owners of the company which employed them didn't know what they were doing. Obviously, everyone who fails to get a new business going does not fall into this category, but there are certainly many people who do.

Nevertheless, despite the woeful statistics, there certainly are many individual risk-takers who have succeeded in establishing businesses of their own. For example, just consider the story of my good friend, Bob McCrary. Bob had worked in the electronics industry for many years and, although he had never earned what one might consider "big money," he certainly earned a better than average income. He owned his own home, he raised three beautiful daughters, and accomplished all of this while working for someone else. But despite his undisputed success, Bob harbored a desire to go into business for himself and I suppose fear was the only thing holding him back from doing so. The truth of the matter was, that with all the things he had going for him, Bob couldn't help but succeed. Unfortunately, however, he was unaware of this because he had never been "out on his own" before. Moreover, he had been raised to believe the "old idea": that a person should "get a good steady job and then work for a pension."

Still, the desire of Bob, and his wife Pat, to work in their own business persisted. It eventually grew to the point where they were actually able to visualize their business operating successfully. Since it is impossible to hold an image in the mind without also expressing it, the end result of Bob and Pat's imaging, was the birth of their own company,

"Pensacola Electronics."

That happy event occurred just a few short years ago and, although both Bob and Pat have worked many hard hours, and still do today, they have the satisfaction of looking at what they have created together. They gainfully employ numerous people and they properly service hundreds of clients located in various American states. They have both earned a sizeable income and the net value of their company today—if they were to sell it—is greater than all of the money Bob had earned working for the other company, for all those years.

Did Bob and Pat make the right decision? Just ask them! Would they make it again? You know what their answer would be! Are they Risk-Takers? I don't think there is any question about that!

Bob and Pat McCrary left their jobs and invested many thousands of dollars to do something which they had never done before. They had no written guarantee they would succeed in their venture, but they were not irresponsible, nor were they acting imprudently. Were they afraid? Well, I have never asked them directly, but after studying human nature for the greater part of twenty years, I feel quite confident in asserting they were. The salient point for our purposes is, despite their trepidation, they had the courage to act in the face of their fear. For the person who analyzes a situation carefully, prepares himself accordingly and then proceeds in the face of fear with the image of success in mind, is a genuine risk-taker. Furthermore, as you are already aware, risk-takers very rarely lose; and even when they do, they usually bounce right back to try again. In other words, risk-takers live exciting, creative lives, because they are living the kind of life that we are all intended to live.

So put a smile on your face, because as of this moment, you too can become a bona fide risk-taker! How? Simply by doing the thing you have dreamed about—off and on—for months, or possibly even years.

In the great musical *South Pacific,* Mary Martin sang, "If you don't have a dream, if I don't have a dream, how are we going to make a dream come true?" It is my belief that everyone of us has our own dream. We all have a vision, an idea or a picture of some great or grand thing or accomplishment, which will float to the surface of our consciousness from time to time. Moreover, for a few brief moments, we permit ourselves the luxury of enjoying ourselves doing, being or having, whatever that dream might be. There is no doubt in my mind that you too "hold" a picture of something which floats to the surface of your consciousness periodically, and if the truth were to be known, you would dearly love to execute that dream.

Well, the simple truth is you can. But in all likelihood, it is going to require a considerable amount of courage on your part. Remember, it makes no difference, at this moment, how bizarre your idea may appear. In fact, you might even regard it yourself as being sheer fantasy. Nevertheless, you can begin to turn it into a reality, by making a written description of whatever it is you would like to do, have, or be. Write out your ambition in as much detail as possible and in the present tense. Do not write it out as something that you are "planning" to do; rather, write it out as if it were something you are doing currently. In big bold letters write, "I can" and then yell it, say it, sing it—drill the idea that you are now going to do this thing, into your subconscious mind. Then, choose a friend who has a lot of confidence in you—someone whose thinking is compatible with your own, not someone who will put you down and laugh at your idea—to share your idea with. Select someone who will build you up and help instill confidence in you, with respect to your idea.

Remember, it makes no difference whether your goal is starting a new business, buying or building a new home, getting a new automobile, a new position at work, setting a sales record, or getting an honors mark in school. Whatever it may be, you must step out and boldly pursue it. Keep reminding yourself that you have tremendous reservoirs of potential within you, and therefore, you are quite capable of doing almost anything you "set your mind to." All you must do is figure out how you can do it, not whether or not you can. Begin to visualize yourself as a risk-taker and then start telling yourself you are one. Become fully aware of the "good vibrations" you get simply by virtue of practising these simple mental exercises.

But before you proceed any further with your quest, find yourself a pad and a pen. Then, prepare a balance sheet by taking an 8-1/2" x 11" sheet of paper, and drawing a straight line down the centre of the page.

On the left-hand side, place a minus sign, and on the right-hand side place a plus sign. Under the minus sign, write out the very worst thing that could happen to you, if you were to follow through with your idea. On the right-hand side, write out all the good things—the very best things—that could happen to you, if you were to go ahead with your plan. Clearly understand, that so long as what you plan to do is honest and honorable, whatever goes on the left-hand side of the page is not going to be disastrous. On the other hand, however, what goes on the right-hand side of the page could turn out to be absolutely magnificent.

Therefore, by creating the balance sheet in this manner, you are demonstrating to yourself, for your own edification, the fact you actually have "nothing to lose." It has already been brought to your attention numerous times in this book, that simply "missing the mark," does not make you a failure; it only means that your plan did not work out as you had anticipated. So even if you should lose everything you own, you still retain the capacity to bounce back, to try once again.

For several years now I have been in the habit of reading the biographies and autobiographies, of men and women who have truly accomplished "something of significance" in their lifetime. I have found, moreover, that almost without exception, these individuals had fallen short of their goals on numerous occasions, but that never deterred them! Indeed, I myself have experienced "failure to hit the mark," on a number of occasions; and I will readily admit it hurts a little and it even causes a certain amount of embarrassment. But be that as it may, it has never stopped me from trying again and it need not stop you either, because we all possess the ability to get up and get going once again.

Therefore, this very moment, make up your mind that you are going to become the "Risk-Taker" you truly wish to become.

Chapter 8

THE
RAZOR'S
EDGE

THE RAZOR'S EDGE

**You are only one inch ... one step ...
one idea ... away from turning
onto the boulevard of beauty
in your own life.**

It has often been said the line which separates
winning from losing is as fine as a razor's edge—and
it is. (I am talking about winning in a big way and in
all areas of your life.)

W. Somerset Maugham wrote an entire book
entitled The Razor's Edge, and Daryl F. Zanuck spent
four million dollars producing a movie which had the
same title. Both of these great men—author and movie
maker alike—knew there wasn't a big difference among
people; there was only a big difference in the things
they accomplished. (That was the theme of the movie
as well as the book.)

One person "just about" starts a project, the other
person starts it. One individual "almost" completes a
task, the other does complete it. One person sees an
opportunity, the other acts on it. One student "nearly"
passes the exam, the other does pass it—and although
the difference in their marks may be only one
percentage point out of a hundred, it's that one point
that makes all the difference.

The annals of sport's history are rich with dramatic
illustrations of the Razor's Edge concept. For example,
at the 1976 Olympic games in Montreal, Canada, there
were eight finalists competing in the one-hundred meter

dash, but the runner who won the Olympic gold medal was only one-tenth of a second faster than the runner who finished in last place.

In 1947, ARMED —the first race horse in the history of United States' racing to win over one million dollars in prize money over the duration of his career— had earnings of $761,500. But the horse which finished second in earnings that same year—a horse which often lost races a mile long by only "a nose"—won only $75,000. Now, if one were to look at their winnings alone, it would appear that ARMED was thirteen times better than his closest competitor. However, when you compare "the times" that were actually registered by those two horses in their races, you discover he really wasn't even four percent superior!

Now, you may have grown up with the idea that some people have it and some people don't. Or, because some people are much better than others, they enjoy much more of the abundance of life. But I want you to understand, right here and now, this idea is absolutely false! For you are every bit as good, or as powerful, as anyone you see, know, or even hear about. Remember, since the difference between them and you is only in the area of accomplishments, and since there is something you can do that will vastly improve the results you are achieving presently, you have the potential to become even more successful than they are. You may already know how to do what others are doing (if you don't, you can learn), and since your potential power is unlimited, you can do even greater things than they are now doing.

The "something" that you must do to become more

successful may not be what you think it is. But whatever it may be, rest assured, you are quite capable of doing it. Always bear in mind, however, that because each person's world is just a little bit different, the something which you must do is not necessarily the same thing the person you live with or work with, must do. Nevertheless, there is no question that you will eventually find out what it is that you must do. So make up your mind—immediately—when you do figure out what that Razor's Edge is for you, you will do it.

Heinz Daues' Story

As I was writing this chapter, a very dear friend of mine—Heinz Daues—telephoned to thank me for an idea I had given him. But before I let you in on what that idea was, permit me to give you some background information. Heinz Daues works for a large insurance company in Toronto and every October his company holds a contest which is referred to as, "A President's Month." All of the salespeople in the company "gear" themselves up for this contest and they each perform at their peak level of productivity. Their reward, if they should win the contest, is both fame and fortune. (The company always recognizes its proven leaders.)

As he does every year, Heinz had an exceptional "President's Month." But, in keeping with his practice of previous years, he was planning to "relax a bit" in November, or at least to revert to what he considered to be "normal production." As I was talking to him one afternoon, however, I noticed that his usual high degree of enthusiasm had levelled off considerably. I knew something was amiss, so I asked him what was bothering him. He then explained he was experiencing a "big let down," now that his "big month" had come to an end. In an attempt to raise Heinz's spirits, I asked him the following question: "Heinz, what would you do with the extra commission you would earn, if you were to repeat your October performance in November?" (He actually earned three times his usual monthly income in October.)

Seeing the true meaning behind my question, Heinz's face brightened considerably and a broad smile appeared across his face. Then I quickly added, "We both know you are quite "capable" of repeating your October performance in November; there is absolutely no question about that." By this time Heinz had become thoroughly convinced, that not only was he capable of repeating his performance, but he definitely would repeat it. He said, with his customary confidence and vigor fully restored, "All right Bob, I'm going to do it."

The Razor's Edge—he did it—Heinz Daues beat his own record of October in November! Think of the difference this will make in his annual income, not to mention his standing in the company. You just know he will duplicate or better his performance next November, following "President's Month."

The "something" for Heinz Daues turned out to be nothing more sophisticated, than deciding to do the same thing in November, which he had already done in October. Perhaps you are saying to yourself, "anyone could have figured that out," and you're right—they could have. But there are a few thousand people selling for the same company that Heinz sells for and I'll bet you "dollars to donuts," there weren't five others who did!

Vince Lombardi, former football coach of the outstanding Green Bay Packers football team, described the Razor's Edge concept in football very well when he said, "Most games are won or lost in the last two minutes of the first and second half." But what Lombardi is best remembered for—with respect to football's Razor's Edge—is the "Second Effort" concept, which he introduced for the edification of his players. In a nutshell, the "Second Effort" concept simply meant, that when a player was initially stopped by the opposing team, he would always surge forward a second time, with the added thrust of a "second effort."

Now, just consider the tremendous difference you could create in your own life if you were to adopt a similar mental attitude. For example, if you are a person who is working in sales and currently selling only three units a week, what would the consequences be for you if you were to decide to make one additional sale per week, through a conscientious application of the second effort concept? Well, on a weekly basis, it might not appear to be a major breakthrough. However, viewed over the time frame of an entire career, it would actually amount to well over two thousand extra sales. Moreover, from a monetary standpoint, it would mean you would actually receive an extra ten years' income over the span of a forty-year career. Yes, that one sale would be the Razor's Edge difference, which could catapult you into "the big leagues" in your chosen career.

Milt Campbell's Triumph

One individual who discovered the Razor's Edge difference for himself, in his own life, is Milton Campbell. You see, Milt went to the Olympic Games in 1952, to compete in the decathlon event. He performed with distinction, finishing in second place in the world and as a result, brought home an Olympic silver medal. However, Milt's ambition has always been to win the Olympic gold medal. Therefore, when he returned home, he gave it that old second effort and he started his training program all over again. For the next four years, Milt Campbell dedicated himself singlemindedly to a training schedule, which would culminate with his winning the Olympic gold medal for his country at the 1956 Olympic games.

In the aftermath of that spectacular achievement, I had the pleasure of speaking with Milt on numerous occasions. He often confided to me that many of the athletes against whom he competed in high school were far superior to him at that time. But at some point, they had made the decision to abandon a sports career and the Razor's Edge difference for Milt was that he kept training. The result—the day they pinned the gold medal on Milt, he was recognized as the best athlete in the entire world!

One of the most powerful illustrations of the fine line which separates winning from losing was revealed in the filming of the movie, *The Razor's Edge*. The cast for the movie was comprised of eight "principal actors," and eight "stand-ins." (That is to say, each "principal" had a "stand-in" to do the hard, gruelling and tiresome work for him, while the stars did "the rest!") After the film had been completed, *Life Magazine* published a story in which the pictures of the eight "principals" were exhibited on one page, and the eight "stand-ins" were shown on the opposite page.

The stand-in for "the star" of the film, Tyrone Power, was a man by the name of Thomas Noonan. Noonan was a close associate of Power's and they had even attended the same high school at the same time. Both men were about the same size, they were equal in intelligence, they dressed almost identically, and they resembled one another very closely, even in their physical appearance. In point of fact, as close a resemblance as was humanly possible existed between each "principal actor" and his or her "stand-in." But in one way—and one way only—the "principal actors" and their "stand-ins" were completely dissimilar. For the combined salaries received by the eight "principals" for the picture amounted to, what was at that time, a staggering $489,000. The combined salaries for the eight "stand-ins," on the other hand, amounted to a paltry $6,534. The "principals" may only have been slightly more talented than their "understudies" were, but the monetary compensation which they received was seventy-five times greater!

As your awareness becomes increasingly great with respect to "The Razor's Edge" concept, you will be astounded by the number of such examples you encounter every day. As a case in point, just consider how much kindlier you feel towards a particular retail store, where the cashier smiles and "thanks you for your business," and then asks you to come back "real soon", as compared to one where you are greeted with a stern, "Well, are you going to buy anything or not," attitude.

Or consider this illustration—approximately one year ago, a family attended one of my seminars in Toronto. They were a truly beautiful family, but they had a serious problem and they asked me if I could help them solve it. They informed me, to begin with, that they were the owners of an automobile repair shop. But they also explained their business had gone sour, so "sour," in fact, they were seriously contemplating "closing their doors," and going to work for someone else.

In an attempt to assist them, I visited them on the premises of their shop and I asked them a series of related questions. Then, I "sat back" and listened very carefully to the answers which they provided me with. It wasn't long before I ascertained, that whenever I asked a question having to do with their ability as mechanics, they answered with great enthusiasm and literally overflowing with confidence. In fact, they soon had me convinced not only were they very skillful mechanics, but they were exceptionally hard workers as well.

On the other hand, however, I also discerned, that whenever I asked them a question which touched upon the public relation's side of their business, they exhibited absolutely no enthusiasm, whatsoever. In fact, an aura of pessimism and despondency actually came over them. It was fairly obvious to me, therefore, the only problem which this family really had was dealing with their own mental attitudes.

Once I had identified the exact nature of the problem, I was able to suggest corrective action. I told them they must begin to "visualize their shop full of cars which needed to be repaired." I suggested, moreover, that every time they visualized themselves doing work on a car, they also visualize themselves vacuuming the inside of the car, washing the outside, and making sure the windows were spotless. I pointed out to them, that because most people don't really understand very much about the mechanical aspects of a car, the only thing which they would notice, was "how it looked," and since almost everyone feels better driving a car that looks good, these little extra touches would soon start paying great dividends for them.

Approximately two weeks later, I received a phone call from one of the family members. She told me that none of them quite understood how "something so basic," could make such a tremendous difference. But nevertheless, they had become so busy in the next two weeks since I had visited them, their only problem now was completing all of the work which they had attracted to themselves. The Razor's Edge difference that changed their business from a loser into a winner, turned out to be nothing more dramatic than a hospitable attitude and a few additional touches on each and every automobile. Was it worth it? Just ask the Jacob's family of Toronto, Canada!

Most educators will admit—with some coaxing— that the average individual reads at only about a grade six or seven level. The reason for this is we are taught to read by the time we reach grade six or seven, and then we never bother to improve our reading skills beyond that point. You should realize, moreover, that what is true about "reading," is also true of most other skills which we acquire in life. Once people have become proficient in the basics in any particular field, they usually choose to stop learning, and of course, from that point forward they cease to improve. Since this is true of most people, it follows that it is only the small minority of people in any given field who will go on to become the acknowledged experts in their chosen vocation. Therefore, they are the people who can demand and who will receive the lion's share of the income in their field. (Just reflect upon the vast difference in the incomes of the actors in the movie *The Razor's Edge*.)

Taking this information into account, consider the job you are doing presently and ask yourself the following questions: "How good am I at doing it?," and "How much better could I be?" Realize, that if you would study your chosen field for one hour per day, in five years time you would have studied for 45 forty-hour weeks, which amounts to almost a full year of study. Moreover, since you would only be studying for one hour at any given time, you would be able to give the material your undivided attention. Therefore, it would actually be the equivalent of "a full year" of concentrated study. This means that by the end of the first year, you would already have put in nine forty-hour weeks of invaluable study time. Although this amounts to only one hour of study per day, if you were to follow this schedule rigorously, in a relatively short span of time you would stand among your peers like a giraffe in a herd of field mice.

In fact, when you really think about it, you will soon understand there isn't any competition at all, because there are so few people in the race, that even the losers are winners. Therefore, you need not do a tremendous amount of studying to gain the understanding you require, because again, the difference between knowledge and ignorance, may be as fine as "the Razor's Edge."

Let's get down to specifics again—as I have explained to audiences on numerous occasions, I do a great deal of studying by listening to educational tapes while I am driving my car. I'd like to suggest that you turn your radio off and your tape-recorder on when you get into your car, as it could make as big a difference for you, as it has for me. You should be aware that those people who drive twenty-five thousand miles per year spend thirteen forty-hour weeks sitting behind the wheel of their car. Therefore, they are in an excellent position to have a wealth of invaluable information deposited in their subconscious minds, while they are, otherwise, engaged in the routine activity of driving. Remember, it is virtually impossible to keep exposing your mind to great ideas without having those ideas expressed in your physical world. Moreover, it is probably only one idea you need to make the difference in your life.

Consider this illustration—by merely moving an index finger a fraction of an inch, a person can transform a cold piece of metal into a deadly weapon. Or, by simply shouting the word "Fire," a person can turn a room full of happy people into a screaming, panic-stricken mob. Obviously, these are both very negative examples. Nevertheless, they do graphically illustrate the important truth, that "the Razor's Edge can cut both ways." In other words, since the law of opposites is at work in every aspect of life, it follows, that if you are not consciously striving to move across that fine line to improve the quality of your life, you could be inadvertently moving in such a way, that your particular position in life is actually starting to backslide.

Let me elaborate. A couple of weeks ago, I was doing a talk show on the radio. A lady phoned in and she was in a fairly negative frame of mind because the reality of her life, as she perceived it, was far different from what she had dreamed it would be when she was still a student in university. Apparently, at that time, she had dreamed of having an exciting career as a famous author. However, she felt her plans had been ruined because she married shortly after graduation and now had two young children to contend with. The children, she explained, were still quite young and they were, as she described it, "under my feet, most of the day." She said that due to this circumstance of life, she was unable to go away by herself to write and this made her feel very resentful towards her family and towards life in general.

I suggested to her, however, it was not necessary to "go away" to write her book, even though it is quite true some writers do go off to some south sea island, just to write. But I assured her, these individuals were in the minority, and there are, in fact, very few authors who devote all their time to writing (or who even earn a major portion of their income, while engaged in this activity). Therefore, I continued, there was absolutely nothing preventing her from writing at least one page per day—and if she followed this schedule religiously, in a year's time she would have completed a good-sized book (365 pages), or possibly two or three smaller ones. Yes, just getting out of bed one hour earlier in the morning could be the Razor's Edge difference which would permit her to realize her dream. Moreover, she would have the additional benefit of having her family near her to provide "moral support."

First Artificial Heart

As I am writing this particular chapter, the media is literally inundating us with stories about the "first artificial heart," ever to have been placed in the chest of a human patient. The *Toronto Daily Star,* for example, printed one story a few days ago, in which it quoted the chief surgeon for the operation, Dr. William DeVries. According to the newspaper, he said that his credo, with respect to surgery, had always been— "Rehearse ... rehearse ... and then rehearse some more! For if you 'stick to' this principle," he continued, "when it comes time to perform the actual operation, the procedure will have become almost routine for you."

Dr. DeVries is an exemplary case of an individual who gave that little bit extra. For he took the time and effort to rehearse the operation on the screen of his own mind, before he actually performed it in the hospital operating room. (Incidentally, that Razor's Edge difference has enabled Dr. DeVries to become a world renowned surgeon, who is destined to be "written up" in the annals of medical history, not to mention the fact that it enabled him to prolong the life of one Dr. Barney Clark!)

Another excellent illustration of "going that extra mile" by trying one more time, is offered in the same historic event. For Dr. Robert Jarvik—only 36 years of age—and the man who designed the world's first artificial heart, is another prime Razor's Edge candidate. For you see, Dr. Jarvik is also a man who was rejected, at least three times, by every medical school in the entire United States of America. In fact, he was even advised by one teacher, whose course he was failing, to apply to dental school.

But Robert Jarvik was a man with a vision, and he would not be denied it. He intuitively grasped that he was the master of his fate, and he must have innately understood the Razor's Edge concept—for he would not accept defeat. As a result of his remarkable perseverance, he was finally accepted into the University of Utah School of Medicine, Salt Lake City, in 1972. A mere decade later, young Robert Jarvik achieved a medical breakthrough, the likes of which had never been seen before.

Speaking of her husband, Dr. Jarvik's wife Elaine said, "He has qualities which are very difficult to measure—he is creative, and that is something you cannot measure with a test." Clearly, young Robert Jarvik entered the fierce competition for a place in medical school, with none of the conventional assets—superior grades, a prestigious academic degree, and a high score on the medical entrance exam. Nevertheless, he did possess those all important intangibles: namely, perseverance and a consuming passion to be successful.

Now, I am in no way suggesting that all of us will one day make medical history. Still, we might resemble Dr. Jarvik, in the sense that our particular talents and aptitudes, like his, may not translate well onto standardized tests of ability. Therefore, like Robert Jarvik, it may be necessary for us to bring our particular talents to bear, through tenacity, perseverance, and courage; and just "one more bite at the apple," may be all that is required for us to succeed.

Napoleon Hill devoted an entire chapter in his classic book, Think and Grow Rich, to the subject of "persistence." He said, "There may be no heroic connotation to the word persistence, but the quality is to the character of man, what carbon is to steel."

In another part of that same chapter, he wrote, "I had the happy privilege of analyzing both Mr. Thomas Edison and Mr. Henry Ford, year by year, over a long period of years, and therefore the opportunity to study them at close range. Therefore, I speak with actual knowledge when I say that I found no quality, save Persistence, in either of them, that even remotely suggested the major source of their stupendous achievements."

Surely you would have to agree there was a tremendous difference in the accomplishments of these two men, as compared with the accomplishments of most other people. Yet by their own admission, neither of these men were intellectually superior—in fact, in terms of their I.Q.— they may actually have been inferior to many other people. Nevertheless, because both men possessed the vital quality of "persistence," their results in life were invariably superior to those of the masses.

Therefore, perhaps the factor which will catapult you into the "big leagues," which will multiply your income from a material, as well as a psychic point of view, will be your own ability to persist. So the next time you step out to do something, and "the going gets tough," just remember that the Razor's Edge difference for you could well be your own ability to persevere. Just try one more time—with enthusiasm—and you could watch your accomplishments go from the very ordinary, to the very extraordinary!

Let me share a brief anecdote from my own experience. To complete this book, I am forming a new habit. Each morning I get up before everyone else at home, shower quickly and pour myself a cup of coffee (which I drink on my way to the office). I arrive at the office before seven a.m. and then I start writing. Since it is absolutely quiet at this hour in the morning—no telephones ringing, no interruption—I am able to write without any distractions and I really enjoy it. By the time the other people arrive to begin work, I have several pages already written, so I am then free to get busy with the other work which I have scheduled for the day.

Simulation

Now try to relate this story to your own situation, for just a moment. For example, if you are employed in a "sales" capacity, consider the dynamic sales presentation which you could be delivering in a month or two, if you did a similar thing each morning. In other words, if, instead of writing as I do, try to simulate a sales presentation with an imaginary prospect, or possibly with one of your associates. (I used the word simulate rather than role play, because the latter usually turns out to be exactly what the word suggests—play, and the exercise often turns into a game. The word simulate, on the other hand, came into popular parlance when we learned how astronauts prepared for their space missions. When they were simulating, they were actually pre-living the in-space experience, as if it were already happening.) Therefore, I would suggest that if you practised your sales presentation in a similar manner, every morning—for one or two hours—you would witness an incredible improvement in your performance, in a relatively short span of time. With a year or two of diligent effort under your belt, you would become so proficient, you would rarely miss a sale. So remember, "If the need is there, and the means are there and you still haven't made the sale, it is probably because you are not good enough, yet!"

A guaranteed way to become "good enough," is to do what Dr. DeVries prescribed: namely, "Rehearse, rehearse, and then rehearse some more." For in this manner, you will attain the stature of a true professional, and of course, you will receive the compensation a true professional deserves. And, although I am only suggesting you set aside one hour per day for preparation, like the actors in Zanuck's movie, you will probably be rewarded many times over.

Consider the following account. Several years ago, I was travelling through the southeastern United States with Rudy Michaud, the Senior Vice-President of one of the world's largest insurance companies. Rudy had some papers out that he was working on, as we were flying from one city to the next, and I was also busy working on a project. Suddenly Rudy turned to me and showed me some figures he had written on a sheet of paper. He then pointed out to me: there were actually individual salespeople, in his company, who were earning more money themselves, than the combined incomes of the thirty or forty people who constitute "a district sales operation."

Do you think these individuals were really thirty or forty times better than their colleagues?— of course not! For like the race horse ARMED, they were probably only three or four percent more effective. But in terms of annual income, there was absolutely no comparison. What made the difference for them? Perhaps they planned their day, while others didn't; or maybe they practised for that one hour, while the others did not. Nevertheless, whatever it was that they did, you can be sure the difference was as fine as a Razor's Edge!

Now stop reading, sit back, relax, and think, really think—what is it in your life that will make the Razor's Edge difference for you? You know what it is?

Good—then do it now!

Chapter 9

DON'T THINK IN REVERSE

Forgive

"That slight misdeed of yesterday,
why should it mar today?
The thing he said, the thing you did,
have long since passed away;
For yesterday was but a trial;
today you will succeed,
And from mistakes of yesterday
will come some noble deed.

Forgive yourself for thoughtlessness,
do not condemn the past;
For it is gone with its mistakes;
their mem'ry cannot last;
Forget the failures and misdeed,
from such experience rise,
Why should you let your head be bowed?
Lift up your heart and eyes!"

Selected

DON'T THINK IN REVERSE

*"Let us not look back in anger
nor forward in fear
but around us in awareness."*
Leland Val Van De Wall

You will never obtain any substantial measure of material wealth if you insist upon living your life as if you were looking back through the rearview mirror of your automobile. Nevertheless, this seems to be a very common error which many people have turned into a pernicious habit. That is to say, many of us spend most of our present moments, "floundering mentally," in the time zone of the dead and should-be-forgotten past.

Let The Dead Bury The Dead

Remember the old adage which says, "Let the dead bury the dead." In other words, what you want to do is to stop looking back in your life and worrying about things which have already occurred and which you can no longer alter. For pursuing that kind of mental activity will never lead to any worthwhile accomplishments in your life. You should understand, moreover, that all of the great achievers of the past have been visionary figures; they were men and women who projected into the future and did not belabor over things which had already past. They thought of what could be, rather than what already was, and then they moved themselves into action to bring these things into fruition.

Think of the magnificent legacy which these forward-thinking individuals have left for us living today. Due to their formidable efforts, we are now able to enjoy breakfast in Paris, lunch in New York and dinner in Toronto. We are now able to live our lives in brightness and light (twenty-four hours a day if we so desire). We can hear the voice of a loved one on the other side of the ocean, merely by pressing some buttons on a telephone. All of these miraculous possibilities, and so much more, are available to us, simply because ordinary human beings—like you and me—have built extraordinary images on the screen of their minds, of things which had never been before.

The pioneering spirit of men and women of all faiths, creeds, and color has been put to great use. Those praiseworthy individuals were able to look into the future, to see what could be rather than what already was, and then they ignored those who scoffed and said, "It couldn't be done." Also understand that all great achievers always expect to do great things and then they turn around and do them! Do not be misled by your sensory factors— we are endowed with the same, basic mental tools which the Wright's, the Edison's and the Bell's possessed, and we all have the God-given ability to employ those tools, just as they did. All of us have been blessed with the mental capacity to gaze into the future and to see our lives in a richer and much more satisfying state.

Therefore, regardless of the present circumstances in which you find yourself, clearly understand that if you can build the image of something new in your mind, something that far surpasses anything that has occurred up until now, you have the ability to realize that result in the physical world. It could not be more clear, that all of us have been "Born Rich", in the sense of having a magnificent God-given potential, which we owe ourselves to nurture.

Just how great is this human potential?

Let's check with the experts. Dr. Alexander Rich, Professor of Biophysics at M.I.T., has estimated our central nervous system contains from 10 to 100 million cells, each one of which has a storage capacity equal to that of a large computer. If his estimates are even close to being correct, it would imply that the human mind has the capacity to store all of the known information in the world—with room to spare!

Other specialists in the field of human creativity are similarly convinced that all people have uncharted reservoirs of untapped potential, locked up within the confines of their incredible minds. For example, Dr.W. Ross Addey, of the Space Biology Laboratory of the Brain Research Institute at U.C.L.A., has said that, "The ultimate creative capacity of your brain may be, for all practical purposes, infinite." One must conclude, therefore, the more a person delves into the potential of the human being, the more that person will become aware of how great he or she truly is; and the more that person becomes aware of his or her own potential, the easier it will be to build images of ideas or things which have never even been contemplated up until the present time.

Now, pause for just a moment and reflect upon the degree to which you have been utilizing this incredible power to improve the quality of your own life, and the lives of those people who surround you. If you know, for a fact, that you have not been tapping into these great reservoirs of talent and ability, then you should ask yourself very candidly why you have not been. For if you do this, you might just discover you have been "telling yourself" for such a long period of time that you can't do certain things, that you have actually manufactured a genuine "mental block" in your own conscious mind.

But, you should remove these mental blocks by putting yourself into a very relaxed state and by then becoming consciously aware that you can do the things you want to do—you probably just don't know how to go about doing them. If this is the position which you currently find yourself in, then you should start getting excited; for the ideas which are being brought to you in the pages of this book will show you exactly how to go about doing the things you most wish to do.

Also, please be advised you need not feel regret because you have not fully utilized this great power in the past. For the truth is, there are few people anywhere who understand the real truth concerning their own "hidden resources." That is the very reason why so few people live dynamic exciting lives and so many people live confused, unproductive lives. Moreover, just on the basis of what you have read up to this point, you have already far surpassed most other people with respect to your understanding of this important potential.

It would appear to be the case, that the masses of people have always lived their lives in the past tense. That is to say, by virtue of holding onto old images, they have limited themselves to only "half a life." Indeed, even as far back as the turn of the century, William James (1842-1910)—one of the world's most distinguished early psychologists— reached the conclusion, the average individual was using only a small portion of his or her real potential (perhaps as little as 10%). He considered this to be one of his most important psychological discoveries and, in this connection, he wrote, "Most people live, whether physically, intellectually, or morally, in a very restricted circle of their potential being. They make use of a very small portion of their possible consciousness, and of their soul's resources in general, much like a person who, out of their whole bodily organism, gets into the habit of using and moving only their little finger."

One might have expected, that in this modern age in which we now live, James' findings would have become anachronistic. But unfortunately, this is just not true. For the sad reality is, that most of us are continuing to live our lives in much the same manner as our grandparents did. The reason we do this, you will be interested to know, is that most of us have never been trained to measure our "true abilities" correctly.

Indeed, during the formative years of our lives, we have been inculcated with the belief that our results in school would be the factor determining whether we would win or lose in life. This notion has been "fired" at us from virtually every conceivable angle, until eventually, most of us have not only come to accept it intellectually, but we have actually become emotionally involved with the idea as well. The result is: the lives of untold numbers of individuals have been needlessly sacrificed, "on the altar of failure."

I feel time has come for us to free ourselves from these mental shackles of the past. Let us, therefore, begin this "healing process," by getting in touch with the wide variety of beautiful images which we have the ability to form on the screen of our own minds. Then, let us begin to actually expect to receive the physical manifestation of each one of these images, in our own lives.

Remember, if we are able to see ourselves doing, being or having something, on the screen of our conscious minds, then we are able to do, be, or have it, on the physical plane of life as well. You see, the adage is true: "What you see, is what you get." Therefore, always look forward into the bright future which lies just ahead of where you currently are situated.

Let me make it clear that I am not referring, in this context, to the things which you can actually "see," with your physical sense of "sight" (that is looking at what was or what is). Rather, I am referring to your creative inner eye which enables you to see what can be. The creative inner eye is that magnificent part of your personality which permits you to see into the vast reaches of the "creative, nonphysical world." (This is the area where all life begins, or originates.)

The past, conversely, is the place where all life ends. But unfortunately, it is also the place where 95% of the people spend 95% of their time (which is, sadly, also their life). For example, it is an accepted ritual in our culture, for old friends to spend hours upon hours reminiscing or harping back on, "the good old days" of yesteryear. Hours upon wasted hours, of precious present "living time" is squandered, discussing people who are dead and gone, or reflecting upon things which used to be, but are no more. In fact, there are actually numerous individuals who spend their days collecting "things from the past"—or antiques, as they are sometimes called. These people collect everything from old match boxes to antique furniture.

Then, there is another large category of people, who consume the majority of their waking hours, reliving in their minds, past negative events which have occurred in their lives. They either spend valuable hours thinking of some past injustice which someone has done to them, or possibly about some unkind remark which someone had once directed in their direction. They bemoan and agonize over past failures, or missed opportunities which they somehow "let slip through their fingers." Unfortunately for them, these individuals maintain such a negative vibration, that there is not even the most remote possibility of a positive thought entering their level of consciousness.

Indeed, the only thing this type of thinking will ever create is resentment and/or guilt—both deadly emotional states. But until these poor souls come to terms with the fact that it is they themselves who have been the authors of their own misfortune, and until they realize it is up to them to alter the course of their own lives, they are doomed to repeat their past failures over and over again. As long as they persist in believing that others are the cause of their problem, they cannot be successful (because, of course, you can never successfully change anyone but yourself). Therefore, to the extent that these people hold onto their false beliefs, they will continue to "Think in Reverse;" and it goes without saying, you cannot move ahead while your mind is travelling in the opposite direction.

Take a good look at yourself. Could you be one of the individuals whom I have just portrayed?

If you are, I would strongly suggest that you bring your mind to a "screeching halt." Then reevaluate your present position and reexamine your future goal. Look straight ahead and fill your consciousness with great and grand thoughts of what you ultimately could do and what you eventually can be. Become acutely aware of the direction your mind is travelling, because ultimately, that is the way your life is going to unfold.

Polaroid Camera Analogy

I have often likened the human mind and the material world to a polaroid camera and a photograph. For once you have "snapped" a picture, the course for that photograph has been incontrovertibly set. There is a short gestation period which must elapse, but then the photograph must begin to appear; and it will do so, exactly as it had originally been "shot."

To carry our analogy one step further, I would suggest that the shutter of the camera is quite like the conscious mind, in that it is responsible for "snapping" the picture. Similarly, the camera itself may be likened to the subconscious mind, because it is responsible for "doing the work." Finally, the photograph is analogous to your results, as it merely shows the world the physical replica of the picture which you have already taken, "with your mind."

Clearly, if you were to take a picture of the same object—over and over again—you would do nothing more than reproduce the same photograph, over and over again. Yet this is precisely the course, which many people set, for their own lives. Therefore, you must constantly be reminding yourself, that if you persist in "thinking in reverse," you will only reproduce the same results in your life, over and over again. If you wish to change this pattern, on the other hand, you must look bravely into the bright future, which lies ahead, and see yourself already doing what you now only dream about doing, "someday."

Patti's Cruise

Patti Moir first came to my seminar, with her parents, when she was only eleven years old. By the age of fifteen she was already speaking in the seminars and sharing with the audience the manner in which a concept in the seminar had moved her from failing miserably in French—at school—to honor's grades (and in a relatively short period of time, to boot!)

Five years later she was working with me in the seminar business. One day I noticed her attitude seemed to be slipping badly and it appeared to me that she was not enjoying herself one iota (note that these are the first telltale symptoms of an individual who is without a goal). So I asked her what it was she really wanted and her immediate response was, "What do you mean by that?" I explained to her, that since she wasn't working toward anything, she didn't have anything to look forward to, and this made life extremely difficult, to say the least. Then she said, "But I don't have any money, so I can't do anything." I reminded her, however, that it doesn't cost even one penny to want or to dream. A radiant smile suddenly came across Patti's face, and she told me that what she wanted, more than anything else, was to go on a south sea cruise. I said to her, "That would probably be a lot of fun." I told her I had done it a number of times myself, and I described to her how beautiful it was. I also expressed my expectation, that she would have a truly marvelous time. I pointed out, moreover, that she would retain the memories from the trip for the rest of her life and she could then relive them, over and over again, whenever she desired it.

At this juncture, I asked her what was holding her back. Again, the same response was forthcoming from Patti, "I don't have any money." This type of negative thinking had been crippling her, by preventing her from undertaking something in her life which she felt was very important.

But the real reason I bring this story up here, is to illustrate that even though Patti was mature, had no ties and had no real reason not to go on the trip, her own thinking was holding her back from doing so. Clearly, she was a young lady who was "thinking in reverse." She had thoroughly convinced herself it was a lack of finances which thwarted her desire, but of course, that just wasn't the case. Nevertheless, whatever the source of her real frustration may have been, it was certainly holding her back from realizing her dream.

Understand, that untold numbers of people are making the same error Patti made—daily—and it is a great tragedy. Perhaps you have been making this same error in your own life. If you have, I hope "Patti's story" will be the inspiration you need to get you moving in the direction you wish to go.

In any case, one day Patti and I went to lunch together and we had a very serious discussion. I said, "Listen Patti, if you really want to go on a cruise, you must quit looking back or looking at "what is," because looking at present results is a very common form of thinking in reverse. You must commence to look ahead and you must start applying what we profess in the seminars. So go ahead and book your trip—make definite plans—and don't give one thought to anything going wrong. Know that whatever you need for your goal to materialize, will begin to be attracted to you, as soon as you accept the idea that you are going, and make definite plans to do so. If it is money that you need, you will have it. It might not all be in place until the very last moment; but if you see it, and you believe it, and you expect it, you most certainly will receive it."

I won't bore you with the details of how things all came together, but I will tell you they came together in wondrous and unexpected ways. Eventually, Patti actually attracted more money than she required for her trip. I was at the airport at approximately 6 a.m. with Patti's parents—on the morning that she left, and it was a tremendously gratifying experience for me, to see her face aglow with nervous excitement. Suffice it to say, she went on her cruise. She had enough courage to travel alone and she enjoyed a trip which she will surely remember all the days of her life. But what is even more important than the trip itself is the awareness Patti gained from the experience. For she now knows, through her own personal experience, that if you think in reverse, you will only see reasons why you can't. However, if you will but look into the future with a positive, even expectant attitude, you will see that you "can do." Patti will be able to apply this awareness toward the achievement of all of her future wishes.

Have you been dreaming of a trip? If you have, go out and book your reservations. It doesn't matter if the reservations are for six months or a year from now; make them immediately and then enjoy the anticipation which precedes the actual event. I honestly believe that in Patti's particular case, the excitement leading up to her trip was equally as enjoyable and exciting as the actual trip itself (not to mention the enjoyment which she will derive from the memories of her trip, which she will carry with her for the rest of her life).

The probable reason that so few people make plans or set goals, similar to the one discussed above, is that most people are unable—in their own mind—to figure out how everything necessary will come together. But you must understand, you need not know how everything will come together. All you have to understand is the underlying principle, by which your good comes; namely, everything which you receive in life comes by virtue of the "Law of Attraction."

The Paul Hutsey story—in chapter three—is an excellent example of a conscientious, intelligent, hardworking person, who was attempting to do something which was tantamount to a person jumping off the front porch of his home, and then expecting, somehow, to land on the roof—you know that this is never going to happen. Yet Paul had spent twenty years:

1)   letting the sales sheets in his office control the image that he held of his operation, and

2)   attempting to improve the results he was getting through sheer force of will, dogged determination and long hard hours of agonizing toil.

Everybody—by doing all of these things— certainly will improve their results to some degree;

but they will never witness a dramatic improvement in their results, until they have first altered the image, which they are holding in their mind's eye. Paul Hutsey is a prime illustration of a person who fully believed he was looking ahead, when in actual fact, he was guilty of "thinking almost completely in reverse." For he spent the vast majority of his time consciously focusing on present results, present thoughts and present images.

If you have been guilty of allowing your sales-sheets, your bank account, or the x-rays the doctor takes of your body, control the way you feel, think, or view your sales, financial position or health, I can assure you that—just as certain as it's going to get dark tonight—there will not be any marked improvement in your life in any of these areas. On the other hand, if you will let the present, physical results serve only as an indication of the images which you have been holding in the past, and then you proceed—by virtue of your own higher mental faculties—to look into the bright future and to build an image of the good that you desire (just as Patti and Paul did), you will see your image materialize. But again, as long as you continue to let your present or past results control your thinking process, you will never live to see your dreams come true.

Therefore, look up, look ahead and form the image of the life you choose to live, then everything you touch or come in contact with will grow and expand and express itself in a greater and greater way.

Individuals who are thinking in reverse, very

rarely, if ever, originate ideas which lead them to providing meaningful service to others. The reason for this is that they are only able to see what someone else has already done. As a result of their limited mind-set, the rewards which they will ultimately receive in life are destined to be equally limited.

The 333 Story

I was doing a seminar, which ran from Thursday night to Sunday, at the Deerhurst Lodge, which is a resort approximately 100 miles north of Toronto. On the Friday night, a tornado swept through Barrie, Ontario, a town about 40 miles south of Deerhurst. The tornado killed a dozen people and did millions of dollars worth of damage. On the Sunday night, as I was coming home, I stopped the car when I got to Barrie. I got out on the side of the highway and looked around. It was a mess. Everywhere I looked, there were smashed houses and cars turned upside down.

That same night, another gentleman, Bob Templeton, was driving down the same highway. He and I had never met, however, an idea from my seminar was about to bring us together in a lasting friendship. He stopped to look at the disaster, just as I had, only his thoughts were different than my own. Bob was the Vice-President of Telemedia Communications, a company which owns a string of radio stations in Ontario and Quebec. As he stood there viewing the disaster, he thought there must be something he could do for these people (with the radio stations he had). That thought kept returning to his mind that night and all the next day.

The following night, I was doing another seminar in Toronto. Bob Templeton and Bob Johnson, another vice-president from Telemedia, came in and stood at the back of the room. They were evaluating my seminar, trying to decide if I could help their company reach its goals, which I ultimately did. Because of Bob Templeton's influence, I subsequently worked for the entire Canadian broadcasting industry. He loved what I was doing in my seminars because it was in harmony with his way of thinking. Bob Templeton became fascinated with the laws of the universe, particularly *The Law of Polarity* or as it is often referred to, The *Law of Opposites.* This law clearly states everything has an opposite. You cannot have an up without a down, hot without cold or in without out. By the same token, if you can figure out why something you want to do cannot be done, by law, you must be able to figure out how it can be done. People who accomplish great things are aware of the negative, however, they give all of their mental energy to the positive. After the seminar, Bob Templeton went back to his office. He told me it was late but this one idea he picked up had him excited. It also had him committed to the idea of raising millions of dollars and giving it to the people who had been caught in the tornado, and he was going to raise the money immediately! Futhermore, he was not remotely interested in why he couldn't.

The following Friday he called all of his executives at Telemedia into his office. At the top of a flip chart in bold letters, he wrote three 3's. He said to his executives "How would you like to raise 3 million dollars, 3 days from now, in just 3 hours and give the money to the people in Barrie?" There was nothing but silence in the room.

Finally someone said, "Templeton, you're crazy. There is absolutely no way we could raise 3 million dollars, in 3 hours, 3 days from now!"

Bob said, "Wait a minute. I didn't ask you if we could or even if we should. I just asked you if you would like to." Bob Templeton was wise; he was appealing to the charitable side of their nature. It was important for those present to openly admit that this was something they *wanted* to do. Bob Templeton knew that his new idea could show anyone how to accomplish anything they wanted by working with the law.

They all said, "Sure, we'd like to." He then drew a large T underneath the 333. On one side he wrote, 'Why We Can't.' On the other side he wrote, 'How We Can.' Under the words, 'Why We Can't,' Bob Templeton drew a large X. As he placed the X on the flip chart, he said, "Now there is no place to record the ideas we think of which explain why we can't raise 3 million dollars, in 3 hours, 3 days from now, regardless of how valid they might be." He continued by explaining, "When anyone calls out an idea which suggests why we can't, everyone else must yell out as loud as they can, **NEXT**. That will be our command to go to the next idea. Ideas are like the cars on a train, one always follows the other. We will keep saying *Next* until a positive idea arrives."

Bob smiled and continued to explain that, "Opposite the X on the other side of the flipchart, directly under the words, 'How We Can,' I will write down every idea that we can come up with on how we can raise 3 million dollars, in 3 hours, 3 days from now." He also suggested in a very serious tone of voice, that everyone will remain in the room until we figure it out. "We are not only going to think of how we can raise 3 million dollars immediately, after we originate the ideas we are going to execute them!" There was silence again.

Finally, someone said, "We could do a radio show across Canada."

Bob said, "That's a great idea," and wrote it down under, 'How We Can.'

Before he had it written on the right hand side of the flipchart, someone said, "You can't do a radio show across Canada. We don't have radio stations across Canada!" Since Telemedia only had stations in Ontario and Quebec, you must admit that was a pretty valid objection. However, someone in the back of the room, in a rather soft tone said, "Next."

Bob Templeton replied, "Doing a radio show is how we can. That idea stays." But this truly did sound like a ridiculous idea, because radio stations are very competitive. They usually don't work together and to get them to do so would be virtually impossible according to the standard way of thinking.

All of a sudden someone suggested, "You could

get Harvey Kirk and Lloyd Robertson, the biggest names in Canadian broadcasting, to anchor the show." These gentlemen are anchors of national stature in the Canadian television industry. Someone clearly spoke out saying, "They're not going to go on radio." But, at that point the group yelled, "NEXT." Bob said, that was when the energy shifted; everyone got involved and it was absolutely amazing how fast and furious the creative ideas began to flow.

That was on a Friday. The following Tuesday they had a radiothon, where 50 radio stations, from all across the country, agreed to work in harmony for such a good cause. They felt it didn't matter who got the credit, as long as the people in Barrie got the money. Harvey Kirk and Lloyd Robertson anchored the show and they succeeded in raising 3 million dollars, in 3 hours, within 3 business days!

You see, you can have whatever you want; all things are possible when you put your focus on *how you can* and "Next" every idea telling you why you can't.

This may be a difficult exercise in the beginning, however, when you persist "Next-ing" any and all negative concepts, the flow of positive ideas will roar into your marvelous mind.

Alfred Adler, the renowned psychologist, coined the extraordinary phrase "I am grateful to the idea that has used me." There can be no doubt that creative, forward-thinking ideas literally breathe new life into every fibre of your being. They awaken a part of you that you never even knew was sleeping.

Bob Templeton never received five cents for the leadership role he played, in marshalling 50 radio stations from right across Canada, to raise the three million dollars for the people of Barrie, Ontario in Canada. However, you must remember that this is truly an orderly universe; God's way of running this show is exact—when you put good out, it must come back.

I shared this story, when it happened, with two good friends of mine, Jack Canfield and Mark Victor Hansen. They were so intrigued by the story, they published it in their book <u>Chicken Soup for the Soul</u>.

I was recently doing a satellite television broadcast for RE/MAX Real Estate with Mark Victor Hansen and he was telling me that, at last count, they had sold six million copies of their book. He also told me they are constantly receiving letters from people who read the '333 story' and use it to perform similar mental magic in their lives.

Think of it, millions upon millions of people are making positive things happen in their lives because Bob Templeton would not listen to the reasons why he and his staff could not raise 3 million dollars, in 3 hours, just 3 days after they began to brainstorm the idea. By the way, Bob Templeton has told me he and his staff have formed the habit of '333-ing' their wants and, as a result, he has gone on to become the President of NewCap Broadcasting company, a highly profitable corporation, with stations right across Canada. It is my opinion that Bob Templeton has set up a force for good that will follow him wherever he goes. Profit has become his second name. Begin at once to '333' all of your wants and profit will follow you as well.

Chapter 10

THE
VACUUM LAW
OF PROSPERITY

Giving

To get he had tried,
yet his store was still meager.
To a wise man he cried,
in a voice keen and eager;
Pray tell me how I may successfully live?
And the wise man replied,
"To get you must give."

As to giving he said,
"What have I to give?"
I've scarce enough bread,
and of course one must live;
But I would partake of Life's bountiful
store. Came the wise man's response;
"Then you must give more."

The lesson he learned;
to get was forgotten,
Toward mankind he turned
with a love new begotten.
As he gave of himself in useful living,
Then joy crowned his days,
for he grew rich in giving.

Arthur William Beer

THE VACUUM LAW OF PROSPERITY
(Dedicated to Aunt Marg)

Nature absolutely abhors a vacuum.

Marg Made It Happen

I must dedicate this chapter to my aunt Marg, in appreciation of her childlike faith in, and her profound understanding of, this most magnificent law which governs one's prosperity. Even today, it is very seldom that I visit her, without her expressing her heartfelt gratitude to me, for having taught her this great truth about "the vacuum law of prosperity." As a consequence of her acquiring that knowledge, Marg and her entire family enjoy many of the comforts of life which they had previously been unable to experience. Moreover, the simple truth is they would still not be enjoying these "finer things in life," if it were not for the fact that she gained her new awareness.

Although Marg happens to be my aunt, she is only a few years older than I am and we have been very good friends since our childhood days. I love Marg and her entire family very deeply. Therefore, it should come as no surprise that I have derived a great degree of satisfaction from sharing the ideas contained in this chapter, with Marg and her family, over many years. It has been a particular joy for me to have had the opportunity of witnessing them apply this new knowledge, in such a way, that today they are living their lives in an entirely new way.

Marg's first introduction to this dynamic law dates back approximately ten years, to a time when she and her family were attending a series of seminars, which I was then conducting, on the subject of "prosperity." Soon after the seminars had been completed, I visited Marg at her home. She, her husband Don, and I, were discussing many ideas—all of which had to do with the subject of prosperity. At some point, during the course of our discussion, the issue of "their home" was raised. Marg looked at her living room, became visibly upset, and angrily proclaimed that she was "sick and tired of living the way they had been living."

She then pointed to the curtains in her living room and said, "You know something, I absolutely detest those old drapes." I smiled at her and replied, "No you don't Marg, you love them. Otherwise you wouldn't have kept them so close to you." I continued, "For the only things we have in our life, are those things that we love or are in harmony with." Marg told me that she had a difficult time accepting the idea that she could actually "be in love with" something she found so utterly displeasing.

By this point, Don was thoroughly convinced that we had both "gone off our rockers"; Marg for even attempting to understand what I had been explaining, and me, for actually believing it! Nevertheless, I continued with my explanation and I informed them, that if a person remains continually in close proximity with something—be it another person or an object—it can only be because the person is in harmonious vibration with them, or it. The reason I could say this, I explained, was that "love" is just another word for resonance or harmonious vibration. I told them, finally, that what I had just stated was a law of the universe. (Whether or not they fully understood it, or even believed it, made absolutely no difference whatsoever.)

I explained to Marg that if it was true she really did detest the drapes—as she claimed she did—she would already have taken them down, had them cleaned and given them away to the Crippled Civilians, the Salvation Army, St. Vincent de Paul, or some charity that would have been able to put them to good use. Don looked at me in a state of bewilderment. Then he firmly asserted, that "She's not taking those drapes down, because we have nothing to replace them with, nor can we afford to purchase a replacement." I can remember saying to him in reply, "Don, please understand, you will never hang new drapes, or new curtains, until you have first made a space for them." "Indeed," I continued, "the real secret behind the vacuum law of prosperity lies in the fact that, by giving the old drapes away, you would automatically have been making room for the new." In other words, you can't get something until you are first willing to give something away. (Bear in mind, however, that "giving" means letting go of completely or totally abandoning, to another.) Clearly, this is an extremely difficult concept for a person who is solely attached to the material world, to even comprehend, let alone practise.

We discussed the information summarized above

for a while longer and then Marg moved herself into action. She began by taking down the living room drapes which she had looked at in anger for so many years. By doing this, she was immediately ridding herself of the source of so many years of frustration. For every time she looked at, or even thought about, those drapes, a very negative image would instantly flash across the screen of her mind. She would then move herself into a negative vibration, and thereby begin to attract more of what she did not want into her life. As she started removing the drapes from their hooks, Don came very near to exploding in a fit of rage. Nevertheless, Marg would not back down, even in the face of this tremendous opposition, and she continued to act on the idea which I had planted in her mind.

Don's response at this point, was to say, "Well I guess we are going to have to buy some new ones now, whether I like it or not." I then explained to them that they should not worry about how they would obtain the new drapes, at this juncture. The important thing was that they would soon have what they needed. The reason this was so, I explained, is not really all that difficult to comprehend; reduced to it's most simple level, we can say that, "people will soon become tired of living their lives in a fish bowl."

For a little while, Don and Marg lived without any drapes hanging on their window. But then one day I visited their home, and sure enough, Marg had the drapes which she wanted, and she had them right where she wanted them! Little by little, the awareness of this great truth had begun to creep into her consciousness.

It wasn't long after this, that there was no furniture left in their living room. Marg had become tired of living with it after so many years, so she simply gave it away. By doing so, she automatically created the space she required for the good which she desired. Soon their entire home had been completely refurnished and redecorated, and now she has it, "just the way she wants it."

A few days ago, my wife and I were visiting Don and Marg in their home. As we were driving away, Linda said to me, "Their home really looks nice, doesn't it." I couldn't help but smile, knowing the background and having been an integral part of the many battles which had taken place, each time something else had been given away. The last time I spoke to Marg on the telephone she said, "Isn't it incredible, what a tremendous difference a little bit of knowledge can make in your life. You only have to learn a little bit, to receive so much." That statement is oh so true. For a little bit of awareness, does make a tremendous difference in results. Therefore ask yourself, what do you have lying around you that you really don't like? Then ask yourself why don't you just package it up, give it away, and make space for the good that you really do desire. Remember, this "law" which I have been discussing, applies to every aspect of your life.

On numerous occasions during the course of my seminars, I have discussed this law. I have explained to audiences, that although almost everyone likes to have new clothes, most people have no room in

202 *The Vacuum Law Of Prosperity*

their closets for hanging any new clothes. In fact, when you hang something in your closet, you probably have to push other clothes aside, just to fit another hanger on the bar. The irony is, however, that many of the clothes that are hanging in your closet, you probably don't even wear!

In saying this, I am well aware that some of your clothes may have been expensive, so you are rather reluctant to dispose of them. However, you know as well as I do, some of the clothes which you have hanging in your closet, are hanging there simply because they don't feel comfortable to you when you do put them on (there is something about them you do not like). Therefore, I would strongly suggest, simply give them away. By doing this, you will automatically be making room for the new clothes which are inevitably going to follow.

Set the following project for yourself and then carry it out, right now. Check your own clothes closet very carefully—as if with a "fine-toothed comb"—and then remove all of the clothes you no longer wear. Once you have done this, simply give them away. By doing this, you will thereby create a vacuum or void. Moreover, since "nature abhors a vacuum," it will only be a relatively short period of time before your closet is once again full of clothes. Only this time, however, it will be full of the clothes that you really do want to wear.

The process which I have been alluding to is a never-ending one. Therefore, it is something which you should plan to practice all the days of your life. In other words, you must continually be "making space," for the good which you desire. Keep this information constantly in the forefront of your mind; for the crucial element in this vacuum law of prosperity is that you must let go of the old before you will ever make room for the new.

Another word of caution: never sell the articles which you no longer want—just give them away. I realize this advice might run contrary to the way in which you have been conditioned to live your life; but you must understand, that "in giving, you will also be receiving." On the other hand, if you sell the articles, the money which you receive for them will be all that you will get, in the bargain. This may sound like a rather peculiar approach to take, but it is nonetheless the proper one.

Please understand, you can never give too much of anything. Nevertheless, when you do give, fully expect to receive something in return. Very rarely will you receive from that source, to which you gave. But, receive you must, just as surely as rain must fall when two clouds collide.

Therefore, gaining a good grounding in this universal law will be of great personal benefit to you. Remember also, that you are not working with specific individuals or with specific things; rather, you are dealing with an infinite power which operates in a very exact way. As a consequence, whenever we wish to receive anything new into our life, we must trigger the process by making room for it!

This "law" applies not only to our physical

world, but also to our mental domain. So understand, that whenever we wish to entertain new ideas, we must first be willing to "let go of," or to challenge some of our old ones.

Unfortunately, there is a very large segment of the population which has an exceedingly difficult time achieving this end. Because of this, these "troubled" individuals often entertain opposing and contradictory ideas, at one and the same time. They live their entire lives in a state of oscillation, thinking "do it, don't do it, do it, don't do it," etc. This mental state is commonly referred to as "indecision," and it leads to considerable mental anguish and confusion. Be aware that "indecision" or "confusion" can be one of the greatest—if not the greatest—cause, of people being held back from accomplishing great things in their lives.

Why We Hold On To The Old

Why is it that we hold on, so strongly, to old ideas or to old things? I have no doubt that you will agree, this is an intriguing question. In fact, it is so intriguing, that if you were to ask a thousand different people this same question, you would probably obtain enough answers to fill a book. Unfortunately, however, almost all of the answers which you would receive, would be dealing with the secondary causes, and not the primary one, of this horrendous problem.

But if you were to go directly to the primary cause of the problem, you would soon discover, that although it lies deep within each individual, it is virtually the same, for everyone. Let me not hold you in suspense any longer—the answer to the question would be as follows: we hold on to old ideas and old things, because we lack faith in our ability to obtain new ideas and new things. This of course, leads to a condition of insecurity, which stems, at its root, from an inability to understand who, and what, you are. And, a lack of awareness of your true relationship with the infinite power will always leave you with a distorted image of yourself.

Therefore, you must reach the point where you realize that your "true self" knows no limits; that in truth, you are quite capable of having, doing, or being, virtually anything you desire to be. But when individuals fail to appreciate this basic truth, when they are honestly convinced that their supply is limited and that their real security lies in money or things, they will be afraid to try anything new. Indeed it takes no great wisdom to understand that they will want to hold on to what they already have, and then they will try to accumulate even more of the same.

If you so desire, you may put this vacuum law of prosperity to a very simple and practical test yourself. Just take an ordinary cup and set it on a table, or on your desk. Then ask yourself whether you are able to put anything else where that cup rests. The answer, of course, is that you cannot; at least, not until you remove the cup. The same principle holds true with respect to a piece of furniture. Therefore, as long as your sofa sits where it is presently sitting, you cannot put a new sofa in its place. Similarly, as long as your clothes hang where they are hanging, you cannot put new clothes in their place.

The identical principle is also applicable in the realm of ideas. For example, if you have one idea in your mind suggesting you should be travelling east, and then all of a sudden another idea pops into your mind suggesting you should be travelling west, it goes without saying that you will be placed in a serious bind. For there is absolutely no way that you can travel in both directions, simultaneously. Clearly, it is absolutely essential that you "let go" of the one idea, before you can move yourself into action on the other. The reason for this, as we have already stated, is that "nature truly abhors a vacuum."

Therefore, if you sincerely desire to receive something which is new, you must first make room for it by ridding yourself of that which is old. This is an ironclad law of life, and yet, you might encounter one person in a thousand who truly understands it. Nevertheless, when you do encounter that one person in a thousand, you will see before you, someone who not only lives in extreme comfort today, but someone who is also moving ahead in life each day; and at a fairly rapid rate of speed.

So put the law to the test in your own life. Use the ideas contained in the various chapters of this book and you will find that the law works every time—it never fails.

Remove The Kinks From Your Mind

God never expresses Himself other than perfectly. Therefore, whatever imperfection does exist, it is always the result of our individual or collective modes of thinking. Since this is true, it is not necessary that you hold onto anything, "for fear of losing it." In fact, the truth is, you will never truly enjoy anything you must hold on to, because freedom in all negative areas of your life is absolutely essential if you are to grow into the truly great human being who you are quite capable of one day becoming. Stated slightly differently, we can say that energy must flow through you freely without any obstructions, if you are to achieve the good which you desire.

At this point you may be asking, "What are these obstructions?" that I have been referring to. Let me list some of them. They include doubt, guilt, resentment, and any thoughts of lack or limitation. They include any negative ideas which have a tendency to block the flow of creative energy, to and through you. For example, you might very well be attempting to get a beautiful image in your mind, which would cause you to feel wonderful, and yet because of these "inhibitors," as they are sometimes called, you end up with nothing but frustration.

Your problem—whether you realize it or not—is that you haven't created the space for the beautiful image which you are trying to create. Therefore, you must resolve yourself to let go of all of these obstructions, to enable you to make a space for the good you desire.

You should visualize your body as being an instrument through which a nonphysical, creative energy flows. You should liken it to an ordinary garden hose, which you may be using to water the garden at the back of your home. Suppose, for a moment, that you decide to water the flower-bed in the front of your home. In order to accomplish this, you must drag the hose to the front of the house. But while you are dragging it, suppose that you form a loop in the hose and as you pull on it— unbeknownst to you—it kinks.

Although there is an abundance of water at the source, the water will just be trickling out of the hose, a drop at a time, onto the flower bed. The reason for this is that the kink is obstructing the flow of the water, which could, if it were allowed to flow freely, actually breathe new life into the plants.

In a similar manner, these negative concepts which you hold in your mind are obstructing the flow of energy which could, if it were given a chance to, breathe new life into you and into your results in life.

In the case of the garden hose, you would immediately investigate to find the cause of the interrupted flow of water. Once you found the kink, you would then proceed to remove it, so the water could resume flowing freely in a steady stream.

Now, be aware of this—the process that I have described for the garden hose, is exactly the same process that you must undertake, yourself, with respect to your marvelous mind. That is to say, you must let go of all of the obstructions that are hampering you—release the mental kinks—and you will immediately find that there is no lack of creative energy at the source. In truth, there never has been any, and there never will be any. The mental kinks which you have carelessly—and very likely— unconsciously built, are actually limiting the flow of the life-giving power which ultimately transforms your results in life.

Each chapter in this book highlighted various concepts, which you must begin to use, if you are to enjoy the benefits that may be derived by simply permitting this power to flow freely through you. You have now read the entire book. I would like to suggest that you go back to the beginning of the book, to compare the results you are presently obtaining in your life, with the results you could obtain, were you to make proper use of each idea. Study each chapter very seriously—but in a relaxed state—and keep acting on each idea until it becomes a fixed part of your personality structure.

Remember, regardless of how the results of your life may presently appear to you, you have truly been "Born Rich."

"God's gift to you
is more talent and ability
than you will ever use in one lifetime.
Your gift to God
is to develop and utilize
as much of that talent and ability
as you can, in this lifetime."
Steve Bow

THE BEGINNING

One And Only You

Every single blade of grass,
And every flake of snow—
Is just a wee bit different ...
There's no two alike, you know.

From something small,
like grains of sand,
To each gigantic star
All were made with THIS in mind:
To be just what they are!

How foolish then, to imitate—
How useless to pretend!
Since each of us comes from a MIND
Whose ideas never end.

There'll only be just ONE of ME
To show what I can do—
And you should likewise feel very proud,
There's only ONE of YOU.

That is where it all starts
With you, a wonderful unlimited human being.

James T. Moore

ACKNOWLEDGMENTS

As far back as my memory will take me, there have been people wanting to help me improve various aspects of my life. For the first twenty-five years, I rejected most of this help; for the past twenty-five years, I have gratefully accepted it. Anything I have accomplished of any consequence has been largely due to the assistance of others. Some of these people whom I would like to recognize are:

Joe Farkas

Joe has become a very close friend who has given me far more than I could ever give back. He has been largely responsible for the completion of this book. Joe has spent hundreds of hours polishing up my ideas, and has transformed a few thousand pages of rough ideas into a smooth-flowing manuscript for the publisher. As you read each page, realize that a lot of Joe Farkas is blended into the ink.

Lois Ward

On many occasions, I have stated that Lois has to be, without question, one of the most competent people I have ever had the pleasure of working with. Lois typed every page of this book, over and over, many times. There have been thousands of edits and every time the page, or chapter, went back to Lois for typing. Not once did she complain. Late nights, early mornings and long weekends, she pounded away on the keyboard and always with a smile. We could all learn something about attitude from Lois. Joe and Lois actually did the hard, gruelling, tiresome work to make this book possible.

Marguerite Proctor

My mother is an excellent example of what this book is all about. She has been a real inspiration to our entire family and we all love her dearly. When she had every reason to believe I would never win, she kept telling me I could do anything. Those positive seeds she planted in the garden of my subconscious mind, just had a long incubation period. I would have still been living in the dark were it not for her help.

Raymond Douglas Stanford

Ray was the best friend I will ever have. Although Ray has been gone for many years and I truly miss him, he continues to influence me and my life. Ray, and his wife Lynn, had a tremendous impact on my development. Ray was not only wise, but he had a unique way of making a person see the truth. Many times he made me angry because of his candid approach, but I will forever be grateful to him, because he made me think.

Leland Val Van De Wall

My teacher; it almost appears as if Val has a direct line to infinite intelligence, which is always open. For almost 10 years, I spent hours every day studying human potential, and yet it was still a puzzle in my mind. It only took Val about two hours to show me how to make the pieces fit together. I have learned more from him than from anyone else I have ever met. I will forever owe him, and when you finish this book, you will as well.

Ben Hughes

A good friend and the greatest center of influence a salesperson could hope for. Ben has probably been responsible, directly or indirectly, for at least half of the sales I have made over the past ten years. That may seem unbelievable, but nevertheless, it is true. I believe Ben knows how much I appreciate it.

Additional Programs and Products to Help You Realize Your Potential ...

"We've both had the privilege of sharing many stages with Bob Proctor. It is a privilege because we believe he possesses a rare and rich knowledge of how the mind can be programmed to operate at its fullest potential. We believe no other speaker alive teaches these concepts so clearly and accurately as Bob Proctor."

Mark Victor Hansen & Jack Canfield,
Co-authors, #1 best-seller,
Chicken Soup for the Soul

The Born Rich Learning System
Are you ready to cash in on the riches inside of you?

BORN RICH gives you the COMPLETE, PROVEN SYSTEM for using the potential you have locked inside of you to achieve financial, emotional, physical and spiritual prosperity.

Recognized worldwide as the most comprehensive personal development learning system available, Bob Proctor's Born Rich System will open your eyes to the deep reservoirs of talent and ability that lie deep inside you. The Born Rich System contains the complete plan for developing the untapped potential in every aspect of your life.

Here's just some of what you will learn in this life-changing program:

- How to successfully balance the spiritual, emotional, intellectual, and physical parts of your being
- Why you are getting the results you are - and how to change any result in your life
- How to use the natural laws of the universe for your maximum benefit
- The most effective way to change any habit
- The little-known secrets of how your mind really works - and how to use them to get the most out of your mental processes
- The Formula for Financial Freedom

What you will receive:

Includes complete 11 1/2 hour workshop on 6 video cassettes presented in 30-45 minute segments for your learning pleasure; 8 audio cassette lessons; international best-selling book, You Were Born Rich; your Personal Action Planner and Goal Card.

The Goal Achiever Success System

The complete system for setting and achieving all of your goals

Regardless of what you would like to achieve, the Goal Achiever Success System will help. The result of a quarter century of research, The Goal Achiever by Bob Proctor contains the COMPLETE SYSTEM for SETTING AND ACHIEVING all of your goals.

You will learn:

- How to bridge the gap between where you are and where you want to be
- The keys to bringing your body, mind and spirit together to effectively realize your dreams.
- The only correct way to decide which goal to work on
- now
  How to work with - instead of against - the natural laws of
- the universe to achieve your goals in the easiest way possible.
  How to become totally committed to your goal so you will never have to quit and start over again. (No more making
- New Year's resolutions or other goals that you never complete.)
  How to develop a simple Goal Achievement Plan that, when followed daily, will guarantee that you achieve your goal.

When you finish this life-changing program, you will have a thorough understanding of how each element of your being works to bring about the results you are getting in your life. You will know exactly what to do to transform your life into anything that you choose. And, you will have become a Goal Achiever.

What you will receive:
Includes 8 audio cassettes, Goal Card and your Personal Goal Achiever Action Planner

The Winner's Image Success System
Transform yourself into a high-performance winner

Science and psychology have isolated the one prime cause of the results you get in your life: the hidden image you hold of yourself. This self-image operates like the thermostat in your home. Once your image is set, your life is on course to produce the physical manifestation of the mental image you hold.

Bob Proctor's Winner's Image Success System shows you exactly how to set your "personal thermostat" to MAXIMUM SUCCESS so that you can start cruising toward the life of your dreams.

You will learn:

- How to eliminate all competition from your life by moving from the competitive to the creative plane
- The 3 stages of creating your winner's image - and how to move quickly through them
- The Daily 5-Point Program for Materializing Your Winner's Image

What you will receive:

Includes one professionally filmed video cassette, 3 audio cassette lessons and your Personal Action Planner.

"I have shared many hours with Bob Proctor in my home. I am fascinated by his depth of knowledge and understanding of the mind and why we do what we do. Listen to him. He communicates so clearly and effectively. If you want to make a major shift in your life, this man will definitely show you how."
Jay Abraham, Master Marketer,
Fortune 500 Consultant

Mission In Commission Income Acceleration System

How to sell yourself rich and enjoy every minute of it

Bob Proctor used the principles contained in this system to raise himself from a modest salaried position to $1,000,000+ in annual commissions. Using the Mission In Commission system, Bob has taught thousands of salespeople around the globe to do the same.

Here's what you will learn in this powerful program:

- 6 concepts you MUST understand before you will ever earn large commissions
- The one thing you must develop if you want to earn $1,000,000+ in income while still enjoying your work
- The only 3 factors that determine how much money you earn - and why fewer than 1% of the salespeople ever benefit from them
- The PROVEN plan for earning six-figure commissions each and every year.

What you will receive:

Includes 8 professionally-recorded audio cassette lessons, Mission In Commission Card and your personal Mission In Commission Action Planner.

The Science of Getting Rich System
Complete Wealth Creation Program

> *There is a thinking stuff from which all things are made, and which, in its original state, permeates, penetrates, and fills the interspaces of the universe. A thought in this substance produces the thing that is imaged by the thought. A person can form things in his thought, and by impressing his thought upon formless substance, can cause the thing he thinks about to be created.*
>
> —Excerpt from The Science of Getting Rich

Bob Proctor and LifeSuccess Productions have created three powerful action tools for turning The Science of Getting Rich into a way of life. This personal growth program is unique. It contains more than information; it is full of WISDOM.

INCOME ACCELERATION GUIDE - The guide has been designed to assist you in taking the wealth creation ideas from The Science of Getting Rich book and implementing them.

AUDIO TAPES - This album of cassettes captures Proctor's dynamic presentation and his deep understanding of The Science of Getting Rich; an understanding which has been developed from years of studying Wallace D. Wattles' masterpiece. Bob Proctor will lead you through your **INCOME ACCELER-ATION GUIDE.**

The **SPECIAL EDITION** *"The Science of Getting Rich"* **BOOK** with Bob Proctor's personal introduction.

The Success Puzzle

Why is Success a Puzzle?

What has been holding you back from living your dreams and getting exactly what you want in your life? Why is success so puzzling?

Each one of you has your own personal dreams and goals—your very own "success puzzle." Now, Bob Proctor helps by giving you the missing pieces to achieving your ideal life. He likens success to a puzzle: in order to successfully piece together a puzzle, you use the picture on the puzzle box lid as a guide. If you don't have a picture of the puzzle to follow, it's difficult to complete. The same is true of success. In order to get what you want out of life, you must have a clearly defined image or goal to work toward. *The Success Puzzle* shows you how to put together the framework to get to where you want to go.

Bob Proctor gives you cutting-edge concepts that will lead you through the Success Guidebook so you can create your own personal success map. You'll discover exactly what you want out of life and how to achieve it.

You will learn:

- How to eliminate obstacles blocking the path to your dreams and goals
- How to create a "success picture" of your life
- How to put the pieces of your life in place to complete your own personal "success puzzle"

What you will receive:

Includes 6 audio cassette lessons and your Personal Action Planner.

Success Series - Volume I and II

More than three decades of study and research has been consolidated into Bob Proctor's Success Series. This remarkable series distills and combines ancient wisdom, the immutable laws of nature and the habits and techniques of modern achievers, into these comprehensive audio programs.

Volume I	Volume II
SUCCESS	ACTION
DECISION	MONEY
RISK	GOALS
PERSISTENCE	ATTITUDE
RESPONSIBILITY	CREATIVITY
CONFIDENCE	COMMUNICATION

Additional Workbooks Available

Share Bob Proctor's life-changing concepts with your friends, family, business associates, sales force or any other group, by ordering additional copies of his Action Planner Workbooks. The following Action Planners are available:

- You Were Born Rich
- The Goal Achiever
- The Success Puzzle

- A Winner's Image
- Mission In Commission
- Being Your Very Best

Being Your Very Best

Bob Proctor and Milt Campbell (1952 Olympics—Gold Medal Decathlon Winner) team up for a winning combination and offer over 100 years of practical experience.

This program is designed to help you create a gold medal performance every day of your life.

Follow the 6-point strategy created by these two champions that will take you all the way to the top:

The Dream

Bob and Milt will show you how to recognize your dream and turn it into reality.

The Basics

All true champions recognize and master the basics that carry them to the GOLD.

The Resilient Spirit

Failing does not make you a failure but is a necessary part of winning. Resilience is the mental springboard that bounces you back into action. Every champion is resilient.

Gold-Medal Performance

Gold-medal performance is never an accident. It is always the expression of a finely-tuned and well-prepared mind.

Today ... Just Today

Today is all you will ever have ... and the only day you should concern yourself with. This is where Gold-medal champions focus all of their energy.

Being

Being ... this is where a champion is truly born. It is the beginning *and* end.

What you will receive:

Includes 6 audio cassette lessons and your Personal Action Planner.

FOUR EASY WAYS TO ORDER OUR PROGRAMS:

1. **FAX** your order form to **800-317-9679, 24 hrs, 7 days a week**

2. **MAIL** your order form to:

    LifeSuccess Productions
    2921 W. Culver St, #1
    Phoenix, AZ
    85009

3. **CALL** our Order Department at **800-871-9715**

4. Visit our **WEBSITE—www.bobproctor.com**

LEARNING SYSTEM RESERVATION FORM

FOUR EASY WAYS TO ORDER:
1. **FAX** this page to 800-317-9679, 24 hrs, 7 days a week
2. **MAIL** this page to: LifeSuccess Productions, 2921 W. Culver St, #1
   Phoenix, AZ 85009
3. **CALL 800-871-9715**   4. Visit our WEBSITE—www.bobproctor.com

System Description	Investment	Qty.	Total
Born Rich (BR) Learning System	$697	x ___	= _____
The Winner's (WI) Image System	$197	x ___	= _____
The Goal Achiever (GA) System	$147	x ___	= _____
Mission In Commission (MIC) System	$147	x ___	= _____
The Success Puzzle (SP) System	$139	x ___	= _____
Being Your Very Best (BYVB) System	$149	x ___	= _____
Science of Getting Rich System	$495	x ___	= _____
Success Series - Volume I ❑ or Volume II ❑	$ 99	x ___	= _____
The Science of Getting Rich Book	$ 12.^{95}	x ___	= _____
You Were Born Rich Book	$ 12.^{95}	x ___	= _____
Good Grief Book	$ 14.^{95}	x ___	= _____
___ BR Action Planner ___ MIC Action Pllaner	$ 12	x ___	= _____
___ GA Action Planner ___ WI Action Planner	$ 12	x ___	= _____
___ SP Action Planner ___ BVYB Action Planner	$ 12	x ___	= _____

Shipping & Handling $7 per item; $4 per Born
Rich Book or Action Planner; Max. $20
Please allow 2-3 weeks for delivery
in US; 3-4 weeks in Canada

Prices in
US Dollars

SUB TOTAL	$ _____
S & H	$ _____
TOTAL	$ _____

Your Name _____

Address _____

City _____   State/Province _____

Zip/Postal Code _____   Country _____

Phone (H) (___) _____   (W) (___) _____

Fax   (H) (___) _____   (W) (___) _____

FINANCING (Check one) ❑ MASTERCARD   ❑ VISA   ❑ AMEX
     ❑ DISCOVER   ❑ CHECK (Payable to LifeSuccess Productions)

Credit Card Number_____

Cardholder's Name (as on Card) _____

Exp. Date _____   Signature _____

DECISION

"Those who reach decisions promptly and definitely, know what they want, and generally get it. The leaders in every walk of life decide quickly and firmly. That is the major reason why they are leaders. The world has a habit of making room for the man or woman whose words and actions show that they know where they are going."

Napoleon Hill

FREE   FREE

There is a single mental move you can make which, in a millisecond, will solve enormous problems for you. It has the potential to improve almost any personal or business situation you will ever encounter ... and it could literally propel you down the path to incredible success. We have a name for this magic mental activity ... it is called "DECISION."

The world's most successful people share a common quality—they make decisions. Yes, decision-makers go to the top and those who do not make decisions seem to go nowhere. Think about it.

Decisions or the lack of them are responsible for the breaking or making of careers. Individuals who have become very proficient at making decisions, without being influenced by the opinions of others, are the same people whose annual incomes fall into the six and seven figure category. The person who has never developed the strength to make these mental moves is relegated to the lower income ranks all of their commercial career. And more often than not, their life becomes little more than a dull, boring existence.

It is not just your income that is affected by decisions ... your whole life is dominated by this power. The health of your mind and body, the well-being of your family ... your social life ... and the type of relationships you develop are all dependant upon your ability to make sound decisions.

Fax to 1-800-317-9679

Your Name _____

Address _____

City _____ State/Province _____

Zip/Postal Code _____ Country _____

Phone (H) ( )_____ (W) ( )_____

Fax (H) ( )_____ (W) ( )_____

Allow us to send a Decision Cassette to a friend with your compliments

Their Name _____

Address _____

_____

Phone (H) ( )_____ (W) ( )_____

Fax (H) ( )_____ (W) ( )_____

A NEW BEGINNING ...
IS JUST A DECISION AWAY!

**F
R
E
E**

DECISION

CASSETTE

Fax to 1-800-317-9679 or MAIL

Name _____

Address _____

_____
City   State/Prov.   Postal/Zip Code

Phone (H) (   )_____ (W) (   )_____
Fax   (H) (   )_____ (W) (   )_____

**Allow us to send a FREE Decision Cassette to a friend
with your compliments**

Their Name _____

Address _____

_____

Phone (H) (   )_____ (W) (   )_____
Fax   (H) (   )_____ (W) (   )_____

See last page of You Were Born Rich Book for further details

**F
R
E
E**

DECISION

CASSETTE

Fax to 1-800-317-9679 or MAIL

Name _____

Address _____

_____
City   State/Prov.   Postal/Zip Code

Phone (H) (   )_____ (W) (   )_____
Fax   (H) (   )_____ (W) (   )_____

**Allow us to send a FREE Decision Cassette to a friend
with your compliments**

Their Name _____

Address _____

_____

Phone (H) (   )_____ (W) (   )_____
Fax   (H) (   )_____ (W) (   )_____

See last page of You Were Born Rich Book for further details

_____
_____
_____

LifeSuccess Productions
Attn: Order Department
2921 W. Culver Steet, #1
Phoenix, AZ
85009

_____
_____
_____

LifeSuccess Productions
Attn: Order Department
2921 W. Culver Steet, #1
Phoenix, AZ
85009